Participant Book
Catechumenate
Year A

Foundations in Faith ®

Bob Duggan • Carol Gura

Rita Ferrone • Gael Gensler

Steve Lanza • Donna Steffen

Maureen A. Kelly

RESOURCES FOR CHRISTIAN LIVING®

Allen, Texas

Contents

Nihil Obstat
Rev. Msgr. Glenn D. Gardner, J.C.D.
Censor Librorum

Imprimatur
† *Most Rev. Charles V. Grahmann*
Bishop of Dallas

August 14, 1998

The Nihil Obstat and Imprimatur are official declarations that the material reviewed is free of doctrinal or moral error. No implication is contained therein that those granting the Nihil Obstat and Imprimatur agree with the contents, opinions, or statements expressed.

ACKNOWLEDGMENTS

BOOK DESIGN: Barbara Mueller

COVER DESIGN: Karen McDonald

Scripture excerpts are taken from the *New Revised Standard Version Bible: Catholic Edition*, copyright 1989, 1993, Division of Christian Education of the National Council of the Churches of Christ in the United States of America. Used by permission. All rights reserved.

Send all inquiries to:
RCL • Resources for Christian Living
200 East Bethany Drive
Allen, Texas 75002-3804

Toll free   877-275-4725
Fax   800-688-8356

Website: **cservice@rcl-enterprises.com**
         www.rclweb.com

Printed in the United States of America

12711   ISBN 0-7829-0765-2

4 5 6 7 8 9 10
    07 08 09

ADVENT SEASON

First Sunday of Advent

Scripture:

Isaiah 2:1-5
Psalm 122:1-2, 3-4, 4-5, 6-7, 8-9
Romans 13:11-14
Matthew 24:37-44

Focus:

THE SECOND COMING OF CHRIST

Reflection:

Directions: *Write your thoughts, feelings, and insights from the meditation in the space provided below.*

Questions:

1. *As you think about the second coming of Christ, as judge and Lord, what do you want to change about your life?*

2. *Where do you find hope and comfort in the gospel passage?*

3. *In what ways are you called individually and as part of a community to prepare for the coming of Jesus Christ, both at Christmas and at the end of time?*

Did You Know?

Marana tha, found in the next-to-last verse of the Book of Revelation, 1 Corinthians 16:22, and in the ancient text, the Didache, is an Advent prayer meaning "Come, Lord Jesus."

In the 1960s, a group of Catholic peace activists in the United States invoked the imagery from today's reading from Isaiah by calling themselves the "Plowshares Eight." They continue to gain national attention through their public demonstrations against war and weapons production.

The Church Says:

As the season of Advent begins, the Catholic Church looks toward the end of historical time, in which all the moments from the beginning of creation to its fulfillment are achieved in the reign of Christ. This forward-looking stance gives meaning to all the days and years of individual believers and to the life of the whole community of the faithful.

The realization that there will be a certain end time, which includes judgment, gives definite purpose not only to each person's history but also to the history of the world. Since that moment in time when Christ ascended in glory to the right hand of God, the world has been on the verge of his imminent return. No one knows the day or the hour. Yet believers find hope in this understanding. We live knowing that the end of all things is held in the hands of our Lord. The Church, looking forward to the second coming of Christ, calls all people to conversion. It is not too late to commit to the kingdom of justice which has been ushered in not only by Jesus' preaching, but by his death and resurrection, and which will be fully revealed at the end time when Christ will come again.

For This Week:

I want to remember:

I want to put my faith into action by:

Questions to Explore:

Prayer for the Week:

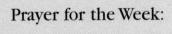

God of Jerusalem,
your Word goes out from your holy mountain,
teaching us your ways,
that we might walk the path of light.
Help us to discard the deeds of darkness
and put on the armor of light.
Clothe us in Christ,
that we might become a people
of peace and justice.
As we prepare to celebrate
Christ's coming to this earth
and await his second coming
at the end of time,
fill us with eager anticipation.
Form us into a people
who walk in your marvelous light.
Let us rejoice in Jesus' name
as we go up to the house of the Lord. Amen.

Scripture:

Isaiah 11:1-10
Psalm 72:1-2, 7-8, 12-13, 17
Romans 15:4-9
Matthew 3:1-12

Focus:

JUSTICE AND PEACE AS A SIGN OF THE MESSIANIC ERA

Reflection:

Directions: The flowering of justice and peace are signs of the messianic era. In the two columns entitled "Justice" and "Peace," describe some signs of that flowering that you have observed in the world, among peoples, and in our relationship to creation. When you have finished, write your own definition of justice and peace, based upon the scriptures and your own experiences.

	JUSTICE	PEACE
World		
Among peoples		
Our relationship with creation		

Justice is:

Peace is:

Questions:

1. *In what ways are you challenged to reform your life and help bring about God's justice and peace?*

2. *What global and local situations cry out for God's peace and justice?*

3. *What are your hopes and yearnings as you anticipate the reign of God?*

Memorable People:

St. Vincent de Paul, 1580-1660, whose feast day is September 27, led a life of charitable works and founded the Sisters of Charity, a congregation of women, and later the Vincentians, a congregation of men. In the spirit of St. Vincent, Frederic Ozanam, 1813-1853, with his friends formed a Conference of Charity, which emphasized outreach to the poor of Paris. Later, this conference became the St. Vincent de Paul Society, with branches throughout the world. In helping the poor and needy this religious society helps to bring about the fullness of God's reign.

Did You Know?

The feast of Our Lady of Guadalupe is celebrated on December 12. In 1531, during a time of violence between the Iberian Christians of Europe and the Aztec Nabuatls of the Americas, Our Lady appeared to a poor peasant, Juan Diego, in Tepeyac, near Mexico City. She healed his dying uncle, Juan Bernardino, and imprinted her image on the mantle of Juan Diego. Diego spent the rest of his life spreading her message of love, compassion, and hospitality. This marked the birth of a new Christian humanity in the Church of the Americas.

The Church Says:

The messianic era promised at the time of creation began with the coming of Christ. The promised "Eden," described in Isaiah, is brought to fulfillment in Christ. Furthermore, God's reign will be brought to completion at the end of the world when Christ has dominion over all of creation. The Second Vatican Council described this time of the messianic era as a time of restoration begun in Christ, and moved forward by the Holy Spirit through the Church, as documented in the Constitution on the Church. The Council further stated in *The Church in the Modern World* that Christ in his life, death, and resurrection gives meaning to all of human history. Christ's work, continued through the Holy Spirit, provides hope for all believers that God's reign will surely be fulfilled.

The sign by which the messianic era is recognized is the restoration of justice and peace. Justice is right relationship between and among God's people and indeed all creation, with particular care for the poor and weak. Peace, which is more than the absence of war, is grounded in friendship with God, centered in human community, and extended to harmony with the whole created order. We, the Church, are called to put on Christ. Rather than opt out of this world, we are to be instruments of bringing about the peace and justice that proclaim the reign of God.

For This Week:

I want to remember:

I want to put my faith into action by:

Questions to Explore:

Prayer for the Week:

Come, Emmanuel, to me and to our world.
Where there is hatred and division,
bring your peace and harmony.
Where there is discouragement,
bring your hope.
Where there is deception and falsehood,
bring your truth.
Open my heart to your spirit.
Fill me with the spirit of
wisdom and understanding.
Let justice be a band around my waist.
Let me wear faithfulness as a belt.
Restore harmony to all of your creation,
on this your holy mountain.
Amen.

Third Sunday of Advent

Scripture:

Isaiah 35:1-6, 10
Psalm 146:6-7, 8-9, 9-10
James 5:7-10
Matthew 11:2-11

Focus:

THE CHARISM OF PROPHECY

Reflection:

Directions: *In the space below are listed the signs of Jesus' identity. Next to each, describe a situation in which you experienced or witnessed something similar. When you have finished, write a description of how you are being called to be a prophet—speak God's Word—in this historical situation.*

The blind recover their sight
The lame walk
Lepers are cured
The deaf hear
The dead are raised to life
The poor have the Good News preached to them
The captives will be set free
Widows and orphans will be protected and sustained
The frightened will be made strong
Sorrow and mourning will be dispelled

My call to be a prophet today:

Questions:

1. *Which people in your life have spoken God's Word to you?*

2. *Name five things in your life, right now, that are a cause for joy.*

3. *How can you take this joy to others this week?*

Memorable People:

Prophets of our day include:
- *Caesar Chavez,* who organized boycotts against the large corporations until better working conditions and wages were achieved for the United Farm Workers;
- *Dorothy Day,* who began the Catholic Worker movement;
- *Martin Luther King, Jr.,* who spoke his dream for racial equality;
- *Jean Vanier,* who ministers with L'Arche community;
- *Archbishop Oscar Romero,* who was martyred in working for the rights of the poor in El Salvador.

Did You Know?

The third Sunday of Advent is known traditionally as "Gaudete Sunday." *Gaudete* is a Latin word meaning "rejoice"—an imperative taken from the readings of this day, especially the Pauline readings in all three years of the lectionary cycle. The liturgical color rose is sometimes used on the third Sunday of Advent as a more festive color signifying the time of waiting for the Messiah is more than half over.

The "O Antiphons" are a series of seven antiphons or short verses sung in praying the Liturgy of the Hours, the public prayer of the Church for praising God and sanctifying the hours of the day. The antiphons are used at Vespers—Evening Prayer—and also before the gospel at Mass from December 17 to December 23. The O Antiphons include these titles for Jesus: O Wisdom; O Lord of Lords; O Root of Jesse; O Key of David; O Radiant Dawn; O King of All Nations; and O Emmanuel (God with us). The antiphons invoke Christ to come and dwell in our lives.

The Church Says:

The Old Testament scriptures recount the words and deeds of such prophets as Jeremiah, Isaiah, Ezekiel, and Daniel. Prophets are called by God to speak God's message in a specific historical situation. Prophets often speak a difficult word, calling people to change their ways and live in accordance with God's design. They also speak a word of hope that God will bring about justice, mercy, and new life. John the Baptist was the last great prophet in the Old Testament line. John is greater than the prophets because, in addition to calling the people to repentance, he also pointed the way to the Messiah.

Christ, the Messiah, inaugurated a new final age of this world. God's gift of prophetic speech is continued in this final age through the Spirit as evidenced in the apostles at Pentecost. Prophecy, speaking God's Word in a historical situation, is a charism or gift of the Holy Spirit, as noted by Paul in 1 Corinthians 14:29-33. Through baptism, all Christians share in Christ's prophetic role. Catholics are called to be living witnesses to Christ by a life of faith and love. In the document *Redemptoris Missio*, meaning *The Mission of Redemption*, Pope John Paul II states that "the witness of a Christian life is the first and irreplaceable form of mission." Furthermore, this mission occurs more through witnessing and experience than in teaching, and in life and action rather than in theories.

For This Week:

I want to remember:

I want to put my faith into action by:

Questions to Explore:

Prayer for the Week:

God of history and time,
you promise a savior who brings
healing and sight,
singing and dancing,
freedom and justice.
Give me eyes and ears
to be attentive to your promise
and action in our world.
Empower me to speak your Word
in my home, workplace, and city.
Speak your promises through me,
preparing me to be your faithful prophet.
I pray through Christ,
who came for the life of the world.
Amen.

Fourth Sunday of Advent

Scripture:

Isaiah 7:10-14
Psalm 24:1-2, 3-4, 5-6
Romans 1:1-7
Matthew 1:18-24

Focus:

VIRGIN BIRTH

Reflection:

Directions: *Think about the similarities between Ahaz and Joseph—the surrounding confusion or turmoil, the message from God, the promise of God's intervention even when it was hard to believe, the trust and surrender to God's plan. Write down an account of a time in your life when you were in a similar situation of perplexity and God spoke to you through another or within your heart. Include some of the consequences of following God's plan, even when it seemed improbable that the conflict would be resolved.*

Questions:

1. *What means does God use to reveal the direction for our life?*

2. *What qualities of faith are evident in the lives of Mary and Joseph?*

3. *How can you cultivate that obedient faith?*

Memorable People:

Imagine the leap of faith it took for Maria Francesca Cabrini to leave her home in Italy in response to the call of Archbishop Corrigan to work in New York City. Knowing little of the language and culture, she and her five companions established numerous hospitals, schools, orphanages, and convents throughout the United States. She was the first U.S. citizen to be canonized, St. Francis Xavier Cabrini, in 1946. We celebrate the feast of this virgin and patroness of immigrants on December 22.

Did You Know?

The esteem with which Catholics hold Mary is indicated in the lyrical prayer of the Litany of the Blessed Virgin Mary that begins by referring to Christ, then to God (the Father, Son, and Spirit), and continues with titles for Mary as mother, virgin, and queen. The titles extolling her virginity read, "virgin most wise, virgin rightly praised, virgin rightly renowned, virgin most powerful, virgin gentle in mercy, faithful virgin. . . ."

The Church Says:

The term "virgin birth" seems a contradiction, yet the teaching of the Catholic Church on this doctrine is not about biology but concerns a unique manifestation of God's power and grace breaking into the world in an unfathomable mystery. The virgin birth refers to Mary's perpetual virginity before, during, and after the birth of Jesus. This belief is particularly significant for the faithful. First, it underscores the traditional belief that Jesus, the Messiah, has only one Father in heaven and is truly God. Second, Mary, a virgin even in giving birth, indicates that, conceived without sin or the effects of sin, she did not suffer the pains of childbirth. Third, her perpetual virginity after the birth of Jesus indicates Mary's wholehearted commitment to Jesus' mission and ministry.

This tradition, upholding Virgin Mary, Mother of God and our Lord Jesus Christ, has been constant throughout Catholic history from the earliest days of the Church. The virginity of Mary is viewed by the faithful as revealing the unique and miraculous action of God in the birth of Jesus, the Savior. Jesus shared an intimate relationship with the Father and he integrates full humanity and full divinity in his person. Mary's full cooperation with the plan of redemption is further revered in this Church teaching.

For This Week:

I want to remember:

I want to put my faith into action by:

Questions to Explore:

Prayer for the Week:

Virgin Mary, Mother of God
*   and our mother,*
we ask you to intercede for us
*   that we might have the courage*
*   to risk everything as we step out in faith*
*   and follow the message of the Lord.*
Just as you gave your assent
*   to the announcement of the angel*
*   and walked the impossible journey*
*   toward the birth of Jesus,*
let us walk this same road with you at our side.
Steep us in holiness.
Inspire us to be obedient to the angels God sends to us.
Complete in us the birth of Jesus
*   to a world that awaits his coming once again.*
We ask you all this, Mary,
*   in the name of your Son*
*   and our Brother, Jesus. Amen.*

CHRISTMAS SEASON

Christmas, Mass during the Day

Scripture:

Isaiah 52:7-10
Psalm 98:1, 2-3, 3-4, 5-6
Hebrews 1:1-6
John 1:1-18

Focus:

THE INCARNATION

Reflection:

Directions: *The images from today's scriptures help us to unfold the depths of the Incarnation. Incarnation means that by Jesus' birth into the human situation, God has revealed the depths of divine love to us. This is the source of our comfort and redemption. Use the space below to write your reaction to some of the images from today's scripture. In your writing, note your feelings and the meaning of the images and phrases as you try to grapple with the mystery of the Incarnation.*

At the beginning of creation, the Word, with God, brought all things into being.

Jesus, Son of God, the Word, became flesh, dwelt among us.

This Word was God, a light that shines in the darkness.

The Word empowered us to become children of God.

Of his fullness we have all had a share—love following upon love.

The Word is God's self-revelation.

The Word made flesh, died for our sins and rose from the dead.

The glory of the Risen Jesus, who now sits at the right hand of the Father.

Questions:

1. *What do these images reveal to you about the nature of God?*

2. *What is the Good News of this feast for you?*

3. *What is the Good News of the Incarnation for the world?*

Memorable People:

On December 26 the Church celebrates the feast of St. Stephen, the first martyr. A martyr is someone who is willing to die for his or her belief in God. Stephen, a deacon in the early Church, proclaimed the Good News of God's coming to earth to redeem humankind and for this was stoned to death. Later, during this same week, the Church remembers the young children slaughtered by Herod, who jealously feared the newborn king and Messiah would usurp his powers. These Holy Innocents are remembered on December 28.

Did You Know?

The feast of Christmas coincides with the ancient pagan festival of lights, during which ancient tribes gathered around bonfires to ward off the long darkness with firelight. Jesus is the light of the world, dispelling all darkness.

The Church Says:

Christmas is a celebration of the Incarnation. The eternal Word of God became flesh in Jesus' birth. God's love is not distant but draws us into God's family as children and heirs to heaven. We did not merit the Incarnation, nor can we earn God's immanent presence. Rather, in Jesus we see and experience the love of God poured upon us in radiant light. Through the Incarnation, God lifts up all things to God's very self, restores unity to all of creation, and leads us from exile to the kingdom of heaven. Thus, in the Word made flesh, we are reconciled to God and offered the gift of salvation.

For This Week:

I want to remember:

I want to put my faith into action by:

Questions to Explore:

Prayer for the Week:

Word of God, Son of God, born among humankind,
We rejoice this day,
For you have revealed to us and to all of creation
The marvelous light of your glory,
The farthest reaches of your love,
The power of your gift of reconciliation.
Draw us ever closer to your heart
That we might fathom the depths
of your love,
Appreciate the freedom of your redemption
And someday share in the glory
of your heavenly kingdom.
With all the ends of the earth
We rejoice and proclaim your coming,
your salvation,
your enduring love.
Amen.

Feast of the Holy Family • Sunday within the Octave of Christmas

Scripture:

Sirach 3:2-7, 12-14
Psalm 128:1-2, 3, 4-5
Colossians 3:12-21
Matthew 2:13-15, 19-23

Focus:

THE FOURTH COMMANDMENT: HONOR YOUR FATHER AND MOTHER

Reflection:

Directions: *In the space provided, draw a picture of your family, gathered at the table for a holiday or special occasion. Name the members of your family seated at the table. Next, draw lines indicating the lines of communication. Using the list of qualities implied by the word "honor," reflect on the relationships within your family and the quality of those relationships. Write about any areas of relating to other members of your family that you need to change, including practical ways you can improve the ways you "honor" other family members.*

Questions:

1. *What do you notice about the bond of love and honor as you reflect upon the ways your family members relate?*

2. *If you were a wise scribe, like Joshua Ben Sira, how would you encourage honor and respect in the interpersonal relationships of today's varied family structures (blended families, single-parent families, dysfunctional families)?*

3. *How has isolation and privatism held you back from helping and encouraging "honor" within the families you know? What steps can you take to become a better advocate for promoting honor in family life today?*

Quotable Quotes:

In an address in 1964, on the feast of the Holy Family, delivered in Nazareth, Pope Paul VI said that the holy family in Nazareth is "a kind of school where we may begin to discover what Christ's life was like and even to understand his Gospel. . . . First, we learn from its silence . . . [and] how to meditate in peace and quiet, to reflect on the deeply spiritual. Second, we learn about family life. May Nazareth serve as a model of what the family should be. May it show us the family's holy and enduring character. . . . Finally, in Nazareth, in the home of a craftsman's son, we learn about work and the discipline it entails."

The Church Says:

The law presented in the Hebrew scriptures flows out of the notion of being chosen. Thus, the commands of God are a light or guide, rather than a burden. This is evident from the twofold instruction to love God and to love one's neighbor as one's self. In its original context, the fourth commandment was addressed to adult Israelites, concerning the needs of their aged parents. This law was based upon the intrinsic worth of human persons regardless of their functionality to society. Later, the fourth commandment was extended to include the relationships between young children and their parents, spouses, and generations of family members. The family is the basic core of society, established as such by God's plan. The Church further teaches that the family is the "domestic church," that is, that God is present in the midst of family life. Thus, the interpersonal relationships found in families are bound together by the love of God and demand honor and love in return. The core of honor is the practice of justice, bound together in love. Thus, honor includes respect, obedience, care, nurture, guidance, and selflessness.

For This Week:

I want to remember:

I want to put my faith into action by:

Questions to Explore:

Prayer for the Week:

Jesus, God and man,
*   your human nature was intrinsically woven*
*   within your divine being.*
You were born into a human family
*   to model for us the sanctity of family life.*
We ask your blessing upon family life today.
Teach us the sanctity of human love
*   that binds all families together*
*   in you and in God.*
Show us the way to live;
*   respecting, honoring, and trusting*
*   our aged parents,*
*   and our newborn family members alike.*
Break down the barriers
*   to forgiving one another,*
*   drawing us instead to love your image*
*   present in every human heart.*
Move us to act for the sake of family life,
*   to create a better society*
*   and a more perfect church. Amen.*

Epiphany

Scripture:

Isaiah 60:1-6
Psalm 72:1-2, 7-8, 10-11, 12-13
Ephesians 3:2-3, 5-6
Matthew 2:1-12

Focus:

UNIVERSAL OFFER OF SALVATION

Reflection:

Directions: *Read and reflect on this legend about the Magi. When you have finished, write your reaction, including your feelings, insights, and revelations, in the space provided.*

The legend is that the three Magi were of different ages. The elder Magi entered the stable alone and found an older man with whom he shared the wisdom he had gained in life. The middle-aged man then entered the stable and found a middle-aged person with whom he shared his struggles and disappointments in life and asked the questions on his mind. The younger Magi entered the stable and found a young man with whom he shared his hopes, dreams, and visions of life. Then, when the three entered the stable together, they found the infant, Jesus.

Questions:

1. *What do you seek as you enter the stable in your quest for Jesus?*

2. *How has Christ illuminated your life on your journey in faith toward initiation?*

3. *In what ways are you being challenged to bring the light of Christ into the world?*

Memorable People:

The feast of St. Elizabeth Ann Seton, the first American-born saint, 1774-1821, is on January 4, near the feast of the Epiphany. Elizabeth, the mother of five children, converted to Catholicism when she was widowed and began the first American religious society, the Sisters of Charity of St. Joseph. Elizabeth shed the light of Christ in the New World by opening schools for the poor. She is credited with beginning Catholic education in the United States. She was canonized a saint on September 14, 1975.

Did You Know?

Gloriously decorated and adorned Christmas trees are a relatively modern practice derived from medieval mystery plays which depicted the tree of paradise and the Christmas light of candles symbolizing Christ, light of the whole world. The tree is usually set up just before Christmas and remains in its prominent place until after this feast of the Epiphany. The prayer which the Church offers in blessing the Christmas tree includes references to the joy of this season but also looks forward to the Lenten and Easter seasons when the death and resurrection of Jesus are celebrated. One form of the Christmas tree blessing exults, "Holy Lord, we come with joy to celebrate the birth of your Son, who rescued us from the darkness of sin by making the cross a tree of life and light. May this tree, arrayed in splendor, remind us of the life-giving cross of Christ, that we may always rejoice in the new life that shines in our hearts" (BB 1587).

The Church Says:

Epiphany, a great feast celebrated from the earliest Christian centuries, occupies a place of even greater prominence than Christmas among the Eastern Churches. Christmas celebrates the Incarnation—God took on human flesh in Jesus. Epiphany celebrates the revelation of this great cosmic event to the whole world. This feast underscores the revelation of God's saving love in Jesus. This action of God stretches beyond the Israelites to embrace the Gentiles. The radiant dawning of light dominating the first reading from Isaiah and the light of the star found in Matthew's gospel indicates the light of Christ covers and illuminates all peoples, for all times.

The Church by her very nature is universal and inclusive. The mission of the Church is to invite all people to share in the banquet of God's love. At the Second Vatican Council, the bishops of the world addressed the Church's relationship with other Christians and non-Christians in the document known as *Lumen gentium* (Light of the Nations). This document presents the Church's self-understanding as a sign and instrument of communion with God and of unity among all people. The Church stands at the service of Jesus' universal and reconciling mission to the world. Thus, the Church is called to give witness and to bring about this unity and reconciliation in the world.

For This Week:

I want to remember:

I want to put my faith into action by:

Questions to Explore:

Prayer for the Week:

Loving and gracious God,
Epiphany celebrates that
your revelation to all people of faith
in the Word
was made flesh in Jesus.
Your light is strong!
Your love is near!
Keep our hearts open to the guidance of
this marvelous light
as we seek and search for you.
Enlighten our minds and hearts
that we might know you and
follow your ways.
Let our light shine forth
as we share your Son Jesus
with our brothers and sisters
throughout the world. Amen.

Baptism of the Lord

Scripture:

Isaiah 42:1-4, 6-7
Psalm 29:1-2, 3-4, 9-10
Acts 10:34-38
Matthew 3:13-17

Focus:

BAPTISM AND MISSION

Reflection:

Directions: Reflect upon the images and phrases from all three scripture passages that describe the mission of the Servant, the early Church, and Jesus. Then after each image or phrase, write a description of what it means for you in the light of your baptismal mission.

My Servant. . .
   Shall bring forth justice to the nations
   Shall not need to cry out or shout the message
   Shall not bruise the fragile reed, nor put out a smoldering wick
   Shall be a light for the nations
   Shall open the eyes of the blind
   Shall bring out prisoners from confinement
   Shall bring those in dungeons out of the darkness

The early Church discovered . . .
   God shows no partiality
   Any nation who fears God and acts uprightly is acceptable to God
   The good news of peace was proclaimed through Jesus Christ
   He went about doing good works and healing all in the grip of the devil

Jesus . . .
   Was baptized to fulfill God's plan
   The Spirit of God descended on him and hovered over him
   The voice said, "This is my beloved Son, my favor rests on him."

Questions:

1. What transformations are possible as a result of baptism?

2. How will these changes prepare you to carry on the mission of Jesus in the world today?

3   Name one specific way in which you are being prepared for mission through this journey toward full initiation.

Quotable Quotes:

"[F]or in Christ Jesus you are all children of God through faith. As many of you as were baptized into Christ have clothed yourselves with Christ. There is no longer Jew or Greek, there is no longer slave or free, there is no longer male and female; for all of you are one in Christ Jesus. And if you belong to Christ, then you are Abraham's offspring, heirs according to the promise." (Galatians 3:26-29)

The Church Says:

Baptism is the gateway to life in the Spirit. This means that when we are immersed into the waters of baptism we are incorporated into Christ, into the life of the Church, and empowered to share in the mission of Jesus. The action of the Holy Spirit makes this new beginning in Christ and in his Church a reality. Through this same Spirit we are gifted and graced to continue the mission of Jesus in the world today. Union with Christ transforms us and carries us beyond our selves, making us a holy people sent forth into the world. The power of baptism is a gradual unfolding of what it means to take up the personal and communal responsibility to participate in the mission of Jesus.

For This Week:

I want to remember:

I want to put my faith into action by:

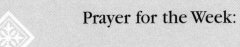

Questions to Explore:	Prayer for the Week:
	God of victory and justice, *you have offered to humankind* *your servant, Jesus the Messiah.* *His coming to dwell among us* *opened our eyes to the light* *of justice, peace, and salvation.* *Jesus is your beloved Son* *who is Lord of all.* *Just as you anointed him* *with the Holy Spirit at his baptism* *in the Jordan,* *anoint and empower us* *to hear and heed your mission to* *all people.* *We ask all in Jesus' name,* *through the same Holy Spirit. Amen.*

LENTEN SEASON

First Sunday of Lent

Scripture:

Genesis 2:7-9; 3:1-7
Psalm 51:3-4, 5-6, 12-13, 14, 17
Romans 5:12-19 or 5:12, 17-19
Matthew 4:1-11

Focus:

DIVINE ELECTION

Reflection:

Directions: *Describe your relationship with God, particularly over the months of journeying toward initiation. Bring into this description the overwhelming mercy of God, your struggle with temptation, and the ways God has remained faithful to the relationship.*

Questions:

1. *Name situations in your life that have given you a hint of what it means to be "chosen" by God.*

2. *How might Jesus' triumph over temptation strengthen your desire to freely choose surrender and obedience to God, especially in times of great struggle?*

3. *Name some practical ways you can respond to God's loving relationship of "divine election"—you are chosen to be a sign of God's love in a sinful world, not because of any merit of your own, but simply because God loves you—in your life.*

Did You Know?

In the Genesis account of the fall, Adam and Eve ate from the fruit of the tree of knowledge. The fruit itself is not specified in the biblical text; however, artistic convention usually depicts it as an apple, perhaps because the Latin *malus* can mean either *"apple"* or *"evil"* depending upon the context of the sentence within which it is used. The convention of the apple, therefore, in Christian art usually symbolizes temptation, the fall, and original sin.

The Church Says:

Our dignity as human beings rests in the truth that we are called to communion with God. The desire within us that draws us out of ourselves into this relationship with God is "built in," as it were, by the Creator. We cannot live authentic human life without freely acknowledging the love God has for us and then entrusting ourselves to that love. In the document on the Church, the bishops who met at the Second Vatican Council described this loving relationship as an "intimate and vital bond of (humanity) to God, initiated and sustained by the divine." However, this relationship is indeed forgotten or rejected by people, through an attitude of sin, which moves one to hide from God out of shame and fear and thus flee from the divine call.

God refuses to give up on us. In spite of human sinfulness, God reveals this persistent, divine love by freely choosing a people, Israel, to be a sign of the relationship that God seeks with all. This revelation was not accompanied by overwhelming displays of power, but by the paradox of a weak and insignificant nation that bears within its life the revelation of the Most High. This mystery is termed "divine election." The Church, called "a chosen people," participates in the mystery of divine election in a new way because of Christ.

For This Week:

I want to remember:

I want to put my faith into action by:

Questions to Explore:

Prayer for the Week:

O Giver of all Gifts,
 you have called us to be your own,
 your chosen people.
Before we were born,
 you chose us.
Help us as we begin the holy season of Lent
 to remember that we are chosen by you.
Lead us to make all our choices
 so that they might reflect your great love
 that the world might come to recognize you
 in all peoples and things.
Amen.

Second Sunday of Lent

Scripture:

Genesis 12:1-4
Psalm 33:4-5, 18-19, 20, 22
2 Timothy 1:8-10
Matthew 17:1-9

Focus:

CHRIST, OUR HOPE OF GLORY

Reflection:

Directions: *In the light of the Transfiguration account, consider the following paradoxes:*

The account of the Transfiguration of Jesus in his glory is sandwiched between two predictions of his passion and death.

Peter, James, and John were also the three disciples with Jesus in the garden of Gethsemane.

Jesus instructs the disciples not to tell about this vision until after the resurrection. This image of Christ transfigured is that of Christ being glorified after his passion and death.

Paul's letter to Timothy states that we, like Christ, Abraham, and Sarah, are called to a holy life. Holiness entails suffering, dying to our ego-self, and embracing our crosses with Christ so as to share in his glory.

Express your feelings as you contemplate Christ's glory rising out of suffering and death.

Write about an experience from your own life in which you have embraced suffering or a cross only to be filled with Christ's light.

Questions:

1. *In the light of Jesus' Transfiguration, what does being baptized into Christ mean for you?*

2. *What does it mean to be "favored" by God?*

3. *What are some practical ways you can grow in holiness?*

Quotable Quotes:

"As God's chosen ones, holy and beloved, clothe yourselves with compassion, kindness, humility, meekness, and patience." (Colossians 3:12)

Did You Know?

The glory of holiness to which followers of Jesus are called is shown in Christian art by the halo. The halo or circle of light shining around the head of the saint or the divine person symbolizes God's light or glory that dwells in the person. At times a mandorla, a larger area of light the shape of the common area formed by two intersecting circles, surrounds the whole figure of God, Jesus, or Mary.

The Church Says:

During this season of Lent the entire Church is concerned with baptism. Those who are baptized are deepening their baptismal commitment culminating in the renewal of baptism at the Easter Vigil. The elect are living this Lenten season as a time of spiritual reflection and prayer to ready themselves for baptism. Each year the gospel of this second Sunday of Lent is that of the Transfiguration of Jesus. This experience of Jesus transfigured presents images of what it means to be baptized into Christ. The baptized are enlightened, purified, and filled with Christ, sharing in his glory.

Christ shares in God's glory, which means both "splendor" and "honor." For Christ, the call to holiness meant that he had to accept suffering and death on a cross. Those of us who are already baptized or who will be baptized into Christ are also called to be faithful to God's ways. Our call to holiness will include the embrace of suffering in order to experience Christ's light within. As we grow in holiness we are assured that one day we will share in the fullness of Christ's glory.

For This Week:

I want to remember:

I want to put my faith into action by:

Questions to Explore:

Prayer for the Week:

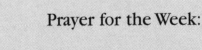

Sit for a few minutes and imagine God's
light filling your whole being.

God of all holiness, fill and surround me with your light.
Let your love enlighten my mind,
*   soften my heart,*
*   and fill the depth of my being.*
Clothe me in your transforming light.
Open me to accept your grace to live as your holy one.
When I am afraid, sustain me with the knowledge
*   that I am your beloved,*
*   upon whom your favor rests.*
May the crosses I encounter
*   cause me to surrender myself to your love,*
*   that I might be molded more fully into Christ,*
*   so that one day I may share fully in Christ's glory.*
Amen.

Third Sunday of Lent

Scripture:

Exodus 17:3-7
Psalm 95:1-2, 6-7, 8-9
Romans 5:1-2, 5-8
John 4:5-42

Focus:

FAITH AS A GIFT

Reflection:

Directions: *Compare your journey of faith with that of the Woman at the Well. The first column lists some characteristics of the Samaritan woman gleaned from her conversation with Jesus. Use the second column to name specific similarities you have found in your experience on the journey in faith.*

Samaritan Woman	Your Journey
Unworthy, surprised that a Jew would speak to her	
Confused, misunderstood who Jesus was	
Thirsty, "Give me this water."	
Denial, secretive, "I have no husband."	
Unfaithful, Samaritans worshiped many gods	
Dawning awareness, "You are a prophet!"	
Confidence is building, "I know the Messiah is coming."	
Ridiculed, "Why are you talking to her?"	
Amazed and excited, "Come and see_____"	
Faith, "Could this be the Messiah?"	
Fulfilled, satisfied, "We believe because we heard for ourselves_____"	

Questions:

1. *What did you discover about your growth in faith through this reflection?*

2. *Name some of your experiences of God taking the initiative to invite you to a closer relationship. How did you respond?*

3. *What, if anything, holds you back from "putting down your water jar" and giving yourself over to a closer relationship with God?*

Quotable Quotes:

"When Christ asked the woman of Samaria for water to drink, Christ had already prepared for her the gift of faith. In his thirst to receive her faith he awakened in her heart the fire of your love." (Sacramentary, Preface for Third Sunday of Lent, English translation prepared by International Commission on English in the Liturgy, from *The Roman Missal*, Catholic Book Publishing Co., New York, 1985, p. 401)

Did You Know?

"Holy" wells are visited throughout Central and Eastern Europe, the British Isles, and Russia. Since the time when Jacob's well was noted in the Old Testament, people seeking an experience of God stop at these wells, drink some of their pure water, and pray to God about their thirst. A large sculpture of Christ and the Samaritan Woman at Jacob's Well by renowned artist Ivan Mestrovic is on the Notre Dame campus. While many sculptures appear in various places on the campus, this one is particularly evocative and inspiring to all who pass by or stop for a moment's reflection.

The Church Says:

Faith is a gift, freely given by God. We do not have to do anything to earn faith. Rather, faith is an invitation to an intimate relationship, a friendship with God. God always takes the initiative, acting first in this gracious offer of friendship. We are free to choose whether or not to enter into this friendship with God, and how we will help the friendship to grow.

Faith offers us a wonderfully exciting opportunity to enter into a richer, fuller, and more meaningful life. In our humanness, the obstacles of fear, doubt, and hesitation block our journey to a deeper faith. Nevertheless, God continually invites us deeper into intimacy and total trust and surrender. God stands patiently, waiting for our response.

For This Week:

I want to remember:

I want to put my faith into action by:

Questions to Explore:

Prayer for the Week:

Jesus, you sought out the Samaritan woman.
You offered her acceptance,
* in her alienation.*
You offered her freedom.
You offered her yourself—living water.
I desire these same gifts;
* open me to receive*
* these gifts you offer,*
Free me from all the things I hold onto
* in my water jar,*
* my need to control,*
* my fears and doubts.*
Somehow, and you know the way,
* get past all of these obstacles*
* and illuminate my heart.*
I truly thirst for your living water. Amen.

Fourth Sunday of Lent

Scripture:

1 Samuel 16:1, 6-7, 10-13
Psalm 23:1-3, 3-4, 5, 6
Ephesians 5:8-14
John 9:1-41

Focus:

ORIGINAL SIN AND SOCIAL SIN

Reflection:

There before me the road forks
* drawn to the easy path, I know deep within*
* it promises ease, comfort and pleasure.*
Fragrant with the grapes of intoxicating wines,
* languorous in fleshy delights,*
*   proffering all desires and possessions.*
But what the cost to others? Do I care?
Why should I not have it all?
* The other more laborious path is crooked,*
* covered with brambles and rocky outcrops;*

confined by compassion's tug,
* steeped in love's caring,*
*   tracked in truth's ways of seeing.*
I am torn in two at the pull and lure of both,
* weakness trembles knees,*
* I am faint with gasping for grace*
and then—
* the light dawns and I can see the righteous way.*

Carol Gura

Questions:

1. *What are the consequences of being drawn into darkness, evil—the easy path of having it all?*

2. *How has grace been present at your most profound experience of weakness and evil?*

3. *What light of faith can be shed on the social evils that prevail in our world? How do you participate in or add to the social sins of our day?*

Quotable Quotes:

Jesus said to them, "If you were blind, you would not have sin.
But now that you say, 'We see,' your sin remains." (John 9:41)

Memorable People:

The short stories of Catholic writer Flannery O'Connor (Mary Flannery O'Connor) offer thoughtful insights into the many facets of our flawed nature. For example, in "Parker's Back," the prideful O. E. Parker struggles with his plain, pregnant wife, wondering why he stays with her. Yet he is compelled by his conceit to win her favor. Parker "misses the mark," for his pride blinds him to reality. A tattoo of Christ on his back only results in further rejection. Your local bookstore will probably have a copy of Flannery O'Connor's *The Complete Stories* (New York: Farrar, Straus and Giroux, 1971) and your library will have many of her works available for your reflection.

The Church Says:

Human experience confirms the fact that we are radically and thoroughly flawed. Our original alienation from God is thus known as *original sin*. We long to choose the good, but are drawn, in this weakened state, toward evil. This pull to give in to our base side is an ever-present temptation. When we cave in or miss the mark, the rift between the Creator, creation, and humankind grows wider. This is known as *personal sin*. *Social sin* is the consequence of our accumulated personal sins, which culminate in patterns of evil and injustice that become institutionalized and systematized.

However, grace lifts us out of this state. Our original alienation from God and creation has been redeemed by the saving action of Jesus. We are born again into this redeemed nature, becoming a new creation, through baptism. While we still struggle with the inclination toward sin, the mystery of grace is at work, accomplishing all that Christ intended. Both sin and grace are at work in the human spirit. We are indeed graced sinners.

In the faith, hope, and love given at baptism, we struggle to live out the grace of our salvation in Christ. Cooperation with the mystery of grace at work in the world is the continual responsibility of the baptized. Moments of triumph over evil systems are signs indicating the as-yet-to-be-completed victory of grace at work.

For This Week:

I want to remember:

I want to put my faith into action by:

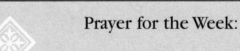

Questions to Explore:	Prayer for the Week:

	Shepherd God,
	    Light of Grace in our lives,
	      heal our blindness,
	      forgive our weaknesses,
	      strengthen us in faith, hope, and love.
	    Shed your light of love upon the darkness
	      of our world, empowering us to
	      bring your light of truth, justice, and peace
	      into the ordinariness of our days.
	Amen.

Fifth Sunday of Lent

Scripture:

Ezekiel 37:12-14
Psalm 130:1-2, 3-4, 5-6, 7-8
Romans 8:8-11
John 11:1-45

Focus:

THE PASCHAL MYSTERY IN THE SACRAMENTS

Reflection:

Directions: *List several events of your life that seemed to be deaths or endings, but in hindsight led to new life. Choose one of the events you listed. Who was involved? What precipitated the event? What were your thoughts and feelings? In what ways did you change or grow because of this event? As you look back, how did this event lead to new life?*

Questions:

1. *What are the struggles you experience in the day-to-day choices you face?*

2. *In what ways does the Spirit help you to choose God's will?*

3. *What are some obstacles that block the work of the Spirit in you? How can you become free from these blocks?*

Quotable Quotes:

"For all who are led by the Spirit of God are children of God."
(Romans 8:14)

Did You Know?

In the breathtakingly beautiful early Christian churches of Ravenna, Italy, one stands in the nave looking toward the sanctuary (or altar area) and the eye is drawn upward to gaze upon the magnificent mosaics of the domed ceilings. Almost always, Christ is depicted at the top of the arch or at the top of the dome and as the eye travels downward, the whole panoply of Christian life in the depiction of evangelists, saints, and the heavenly vision of a "new Eden" or new life through baptismal waters is presented. Through simple architectural placement, one's eyes come to rest upon the altar table. In the use of artistry and architecture the sacraments celebrated in these spaces and the spaces themselves convey the holy and saving action of Christ.

The Church Says:

The paschal mystery includes the entire saving event of Jesus' suffering, death, entombment, resurrection, ascension, and sending of the Spirit. Jesus' paschal mystery is _the_ saving event experienced by Christians. Through this paschal mystery the redemption of God in Christ is opened for all humankind. In the sacraments the saving grace of Jesus' entire life and death, resurrection and ascension to glory are communicated to believers today. Through the Church, the believer is incorporated into the very life of Christ in the celebration of the sacraments.

The Second Vatican Council, in the document on the Sacred Liturgy, teaches, "Thus, for well-disposed members of the faithful, the liturgy of the sacraments and sacramentals sanctifies almost every event of their lives with divine grace which flows from the passion, death and resurrection of Christ." The sacraments have been described by one contemporary author as "doors to the sacred." The presence of Christ is not only expressed, but also tangibly communicated in the way in which they are celebrated. Through the sacraments we encounter the source of all salvation, the redeeming Christ.

For This Week:

I want to remember:

I want to put my faith into action by:

Questions to Explore:

Prayer for the Week:

Compassionate God,
  you gave us the greatest gift of love,
    your Son, Jesus,
  who chose to come among us as a human
    person.
Through his life, death, resurrection,
  and the outpouring of the Holy Spirit,
  he won for us our salvation.
We are grateful for his willingness to die on the
  cross
  in order to rise again to new life,
    opening the doors to the sacred for us,
    believers in Christ's victory over death.
Help us to follow in his footsteps
  so that we, too,
  might embrace death to sin
  in order to be raised up to new life. Amen.

Passion Sunday (Palm Sunday)

Scripture:

Isaiah 50:4–7
Psalm 22:8–9, 17–18, 19–20, 23–24
Philippians 2:6–11
Matthew 16:14–27:66

Focus:

CHRIST'S OBEDIENCE AS A MODEL FOR BELIEVERS

Reflection:

Directions: *Compare and contrast these images of the Suffering Servant and Jesus taken from the first two readings of the Passion Sunday liturgy. Contemplate the significance of these poetic descriptions. Think about your own life; your struggles and sufferings. In the third column indicate how you participate in the redemptive action of Christ by your own willingness to follow God's plan in your life.*

ISAIAH	PHILIPPIANS	YOUR LIFE
The Suffering Servant speaks to the weary— a rousing word	*Jesus' name is above all others*	
He opens my ears that I might hear	*He was obedient unto death*	
I have not rebelled	*He took the form of a slave*	
I have not turned back	*Christ did not grasp at equality with God*	
I did not shield my face	*He humbled himself*	
God is my help	*He is in the form of God*	
I have set my face like flint	*Every tongue confesses that Jesus Christ is Lord*	
I shall not be put to shame	*Every knee bends before him*	

Questions:

1. *From your reflection and the description of Jesus' passion and death in Matthew's gospel, name specific evidence of Jesus' obedience to God's plan for our salvation.*

2. *How has your obedience or willingness to accept God's plan for your life transformed difficulties into blessings?*

3. *Based upon your reflection on Jesus' obedience and the root meaning of obedience, "to hear," how can you better hear God's will in your life?*

Quotable Quotes:

"Therefore be imitators of God, as beloved children, and live in love, as Christ loved us and gave himself up for us, a fragrant offering and sacrifice to God." (Ephesians 5:1-2)

Did You Know?

"The Taking of Christ," a painting by Caravaggio, is described by Sister Wendy Beckett as follows: "The taking of Christ is a violent picture . . . the disciples flee in open-mouthed terror, the soldiers surge forward angrily intent on seizure, Judas grasps his Lord grimly and terribly, intent upon betrayal. Only Jesus stays quiet, surrendering himself to his passion. . . . Only a willing surrender to love can truly 'take' us. . . ." (*The Mystery of Love*, Sr. Wendy Beckett (New York: HarperCollins Publishers Inc., 1996, p 68) Think about how you imitate the serenity of Christ in times of terror, anger, or betrayal.

The Church Says:

That God offered his only begotten Son to suffer and redeem fallen humanity is the ultimate revelation of the depths of God's love for humankind. In Jesus, the human and divine come together in complete obedience, without restraint. Christ suffered and died for all without exception. This willing action of Jesus opens the way for us to live a new life in wholeness and holiness. We are thus redeemed, lifted out of the mire of sin, because of Jesus' obedience to the will of the Father. Through and in Jesus' sacrifice, our sufferings, pains, and struggles are also transformed. As we join our suffering to Christ's redemptive action in the world, we continue the unfolding redemption of the world. Christ is our model of obedience to the will of God, in all things.

For This Week:

I want to remember:

I want to put my faith into action by:

Questions to Explore:

Prayer for the Week:

Suffering Servant,
*   Innocent Lamb of God, Jesus our Lord,*
You who walked the triumphal
*   road into Jerusalem, keep us*
mindful that our triumphs are temporary.
You who obeyed your Abba
*   even through that anguished passion*
*   and tortuous death on a cross,*
help us in our times of pain and anguish, and
*   especially in our death.*
Let us find in you a source of strength
*   that fills us with courage*
*   to face the plan of Abba*
as we live, breathe, and walk this earth.
Help and guide us as we strive to imitate
*   you in attitude—mind and heart—*
*   and in our every action. Amen.*

EASTER SEASON

Easter Sunday

Scripture:

Acts 10:34, 37-43
Psalm 118:1-2, 16-17, 22-23
Colossians 3:1-4 or 5:6-8
John 20:1-9

Focus:

"ON THE THIRD DAY HE ROSE AGAIN, IN FULFILLMENT OF THE SCRIPTURES . . ."

Reflection:

Directions: Think about your experiences of Easter. In the space below, describe your earliest understanding of the meaning of Easter and compare it to your understanding today. Name some people and events that have influenced your understanding.

Questions:

1. *Why is the resurrection of Jesus such good news?*

2. *What does it mean for you to say, "I believe that Jesus has truly risen"?*

3. *What does the resurrection mean in your life?*

Did You Know?

In pre-Christian times, the egg became a symbol of spring and fertility—something living comes forth from a seemingly "dead" shell. The custom of decorating special Easter eggs evolved soon after Christianity found a foothold in northern Europe and Asia. Eggs were included in the Lenten fast and for this reason they were also associated with the Easter season. Easter eggs were mostly colored with vegetable dyes. The Syrians and Greeks dyed the eggs crimson to suggest the blood of Christ. Slavic Easter eggs are lavishly and painstakingly decorated. Armenian Easter eggs are decorated with hand-painted religious pictures or scenes. In Germany, Easter eggs are hung from trees and bushes.

The Church Says:

The unconditional and overwhelming love of God for us, made visible in the birth of his only Son, does not disappear and fade with the death of Jesus on the cross. God's love transcends the tomb by raising Jesus from death. The resurrection of Jesus is a passing over from death into a new life, a new existence. By his resurrection, Jesus breaks the chains of sin and death that hold the human race captive. Just as God took on our humanity in the Incarnation, the birth of Jesus, so too the resurrection of Jesus was accomplished in a real human body.

Jesus' resurrection is an actual historical event and not a psychological or spiritual experience of the disciples. Those first disciples witnessed something totally unexpected and surprising when they found the empty tomb. Later, as they experienced the Risen Lord eating and drinking in their presence, they gradually understood that he had truly risen. In understanding this, they were compelled by the Holy Spirit to proclaim the Good News of the resurrection, even to the point of being martyred (put to death) for their faith. We, too, are transformed by the power of the resurrection, particularly through the sacraments of baptism and the Eucharist.

For This Week:

I want to remember:

I want to put my faith into action by:

Questions to Explore:

Prayer for the Week:

Christians, to the Paschal Victim
*   Offer your thankful praises!*
A Lamb the sheep redeems; Christ, who only is sinless,
*   Reconciles sinners to the Father.*
Death and life have contended in that combat
*   stupendous:*
The Prince of Life, who died, reigns immortal.
Speak Mary, declaring
*   What you saw, wayfaring.*
"The tomb of Christ, who is living,
*   The glory of Jesus' resurrection;*
Bright angels attesting,
The shroud and napkin resting.
Yes, Christ my hope is arisen:
*   To Galilee he goes before you."*
Christ indeed from death is risen, our new life
*   obtaining.*
Have mercy, victor King, ever reigning! Amen.
*   Alleluia.*
*   (Sequence for Easter Sunday)*

Second Sunday of Easter

Scripture:

Acts 2:42-47
Psalm 118:2-4, 13-15, 22-24
1 Peter 1:3-9
John 20:19-31

Focus:

FAITH

Reflection:

Directions: *In the space below, chart out the development of your faith in Jesus. Begin by looking back over your life and recalling events, people, and your inner experiences of Jesus. In the space beside each stage in your life, write a brief description of what you believed about Jesus and the influences of others upon that belief.*

EARLY CHILDHOOD—first memories (ages 1-7)
  My belief in Jesus was
  I was influenced by

SCHOOL AGE (ages 8-12)
  My belief in Jesus was
  I was influenced by

ADOLESCENCE (ages 13-19)
  My belief in Jesus was
  I was influenced by

YOUNG ADULTHOOD (ages 20-30)
  My belief in Jesus was
  I was influenced by

ADULTHOOD (ages 31-45)
  My belief in Jesus was
  I was influenced by

MIDDLE AGE (ages 46-55)
  My belief in Jesus was
  I was influenced by

SENIOR YEARS (ages 56-up)
  My belief in Jesus was
  I was influenced by

Questions:

1. *How has your belief in Jesus changed from "knowing about" Jesus to "experiencing" the Risen Jesus? What caused this transformation?*

2. *How does your belief in Jesus alleviate your daily fears?*

3. *What response does faith in Jesus call forth from within you? How can you continue Jesus' saving work? How are you challenged to be a reconciler?*

Memorable People:

John refers to St. Thomas in his gospel on three major junctures: The apostle is referred to in John 11:16 where he promises to follow Jesus to Bethany and die. He asks Jesus about the "way" to God in John 14:5-6. And, finally, in John 20:24-29, Thomas moves from doubt to faith through his encounter with the Risen Christ. Thomas' relics are venerated in Ortona, Italy. His feast day is July 3.

Did You Know?

The Hebrew word for faith implies something "solid" or "trustworthy" to which we pledge our loyalty. The word "amen" comes from a Hebrew word for faith (aman). In this light faith is understood as believing in a person, a relationship of trust.

In the Blessing of Parents in the Rite of Baptism for Children, the Church prays that parents, who are the first teachers of their child in the ways of faith, will be "the best of teachers, bearing witness to the faith by what they say and do."

The Church Says:

Faith invites us into a relationship of love with God. God is fully revealed through Jesus, who embodies divine love and who communicates that love to us by his life, mission, and in his suffering, death, and resurrection. Faith is a free gift of God that invites our free response. The gift of faith is, therefore, a relationship through which we trust the truth of that which has been revealed in Jesus Christ, handed down by the first witnesses, and passed down to us through the ages by the Church. This heritage of faith is entrusted to the whole Church. Catholics understand this sacred deposit of faith is contained in both Scripture and Tradition. The function of authoritative Church teaching is to explain and guard this deposit of faith.

Through baptism we are born into, nourished by, and made members of this living tradition of faith. As believers in the Risen Lord, we walk by the light of faith. This relationship of faith in the living God can be shaken. We experience evil, suffering, and injustice. We question God, we doubt, we are afraid, and we struggle in our belief. It is through these times of discord that the believer grows more deeply in faith. The faith community of the parish offers support and guidance to believers, particularly during times of difficulty and struggle.

For This Week:

I want to remember:

I want to put my faith into action by:

Questions to Explore:

Prayer for the Week:

*God, I rejoice in the faith you have given me.
Help me guard and protect your gift of faith
    through love of others
    and a commitment to prayer.
Strengthen my faith in times of fear and doubt.
Purify my faith more precious than gold,
    as I pass through the fires of suffering and
    anguish.
Keep my eyes fixed on you
    that my heart will know you are truly
    my Lord and my God.
You have graciously gifted me
    with this community of faith
    to support and nourish the seed of faith
    you have planted in my soul.
May your Spirit breathe upon me
    and empower me to support and encourage
    your gift of faith in others. Amen.*

Third Sunday of Easter

Scripture:

Acts 2:14, 22-33
Psalm 16:1-2, 5, 7-8, 9-10, 11
1 Peter 1:17-21
Luke 24:13-35

Focus:

THE CELEBRATION OF THE EUCHARIST

Reflection:

Directions: *In the spaces provided write about your experiences on your journey of faith that are similar to those of the two disciples traveling to Emmaus.*

They misunderstood the events that had occurred and felt despondent.

A stranger joined them as they expressed their disappointment: "We had hoped. . . ."

The stranger explained the meaning of the scriptures, opening up a deeper level of meaning.

They wanted him to remain with them: "Stay with us."

He, too, blessed, broke, and gave them the bread.

Their eyes were opened, they recognized him.

In hindsight, they recalled his sharing and their hearts burned within them.

They hurried back to share this encounter with the others.

Questions:

1. *How open are you to "recognize" the Lord in your midst? What happened when you did?*

2. *What does it mean to "abide" with Jesus?*

3. *How does the presence of Jesus help you in living out your faith?*

Quotable Quotes:

"*Then they told what had happened on the road, and how he had been made known to them in the breaking of the bread.*" (Luke 24:35)

Memorable People:

The feast of the great Doctor of the Church, Catherine of Siena is celebrated on April 30. Catherine was remarkable in her abilities to mediate Church disputes, her prolific writings and her deep union with Christ. Her zeal for the Church and her great faith made her a reconciler who restored peace during a time of political and papal discord.

The Church Says:

The Eucharist is central to the Christian life. Christians live their faith throughout the week. They come together on Sunday to celebrate their life as Eucharist. In the liturgy the believer is blessed and nourished, offers thanks for God's gracious gifts, and is sent forth to carry on the mission of Jesus, bringing Good News to the world. The eucharistic celebration has two parts: the Liturgy of the Word and the Liturgy of the Eucharist. In the first part, those gathered hear and respond to the Word of God proclaimed and preached. In the Liturgy of the Eucharist, the assembly gives thanks and remembers God's blessings and the abiding presence of Christ in the meal of his body and blood. Together these parts form one single act of worship. The Mass is both a meal and a sacrifice. Christ is truly present in four ways at the eucharistic celebration. Through the action of the Holy Spirit the gifts of bread and wine are transformed into the body and blood of Christ. Furthermore, Christ is present in the gathered assembly, in the proclamation of the Word, and in the presider.

For This Week:

I want to remember:

I want to put my faith into action by:

Questions to Explore:

Prayer for the Week:

Gracious and ever loving God,
you make us into your holy people
and call us to be the body of Christ.
Open us to hear and know you
in the stories of faith
found in the sacred scriptures
and in the lives of the faithful
present in this community.
Open our eyes to recognize you
each day as we carry forth
your mission to the world.
Feed us and nourish us
so that we may go out
and witness to your saving acts
in this world so in need of Good News.
Amen.

Fourth Sunday of Easter

Scripture:

Acts 2:14, 36-41
Psalm 23:1-3, 3-4, 5, 6
1 Peter 2:20-25
John 10:1-10

Focus:

JESUS, THE GOOD SHEPHERD

Reflection:

Directions: *Think about these images of the Good Shepherd. When you are ready, write a description of who Jesus is for you.*

The Good Shepherd: *knows each sheep intimately, each one recognizes his call, leads the flock, lays down forming a gate to guard the sheep, would give up his life for the sheep, will painstakingly search for a lost sheep, finds good pastures (food) for the sheep, leads the sheep to quenching waters, protects the sheep from all harm, provides all that the sheep need.*

Questions:

1. *How can you take on the qualities of the Good Shepherd, whom you follow?*

2. *How can you come to know the Good Shepherd more intimately?*

3. *What ways will you need to reform your life as a result of this relationship with the Good Shepherd?*

Did You Know?

Contemporary scripture scholar Sofia Cavalletti and her colleagues have developed a catechetical method using the parable of the Good Shepherd with children worldwide. Cavalletti writes, "Once begun, the relationship with the Good Shepherd never ceases; the parable will grow slowly with the child, revealing its other aspects and satisfying the needs of the older child, adolescent and adult. . . . The development is from the love that protects, to the love that forgives, and finally, to the *imitatio Christi* . . . [that is, its dynamic unfolds as] early childhood, sensitive period for protection; later childhood, moral sensitive period; adolescence, sensitive period for heroism."

The Church Says:

Like the many titles for Jesus (bread of life, the way, truth, and life, and light of the world) the Good Shepherd offers us another facet for understanding the mystery of Jesus. The image of shepherd suggests Jesus is a caring companion, a leader who willingly lays down his life for his flock, and a voice to be followed. For those who recognize his voice, the Good Shepherd promises safe pastures and protection from harm. The Church teaches that the image of the Good Shepherd illustrates the close connection between believers and the Lord in the documents of the Second Vatican Council.

The disciple through baptism is challenged, as was Peter, to become a leader, a Good Shepherd for others. Upon forgiving Peter for his triple denial, Jesus thrice calls Peter to "feed my lambs" and "tend my sheep," indicating the mission of all believers. Thus, the model of the Good Shepherd has been traditionally used to indicate the role of the pastor and other pastoral leaders in the Church. St. Gregory, in the sixth century, challenged his hearers, preaching, "Ask yourself whether you belong to [Jesus'] flock, whether you know him, whether the light of his truth shines in your minds. I assure you that it is not by faith that you will come to know him, but by love; not by mere conviction, but by action."

For This Week:

I want to remember:

I want to put my faith into action by:

Questions to Explore:

Prayer for the Week:

Jesus our Shepherd,
lead us out of our wanderings,
set us on the path of holiness.
Guard us against the lure
of easy answers and quick fixes,
strengthen us instead
with patient endurance
as we struggle to know you.
Attune us that we might recognize
your voice and follow you.
Light our path each day.
Open our hearts
that we might come to know you
by loving you and
imitating your shepherding ways
as we witness
your Good News. Amen.

Fifth Sunday of Easter

Scripture:

Acts 6:1-7
Psalm 33:1-2, 4-5, 18-19
1 Peter 2:4-9
John 14:1-12

Reflection:

Directions: *In the space below describe what it means for you to be baptized into the "royal priesthood" of this holy People of God. Use the newsprint ideas of the qualities of priesthood to help you write your description.*

Questions:

1. *Name some concrete ways to become more involved in outreach to the poor, the hungry, or the homeless.*

2. *How has Jesus been the "Way" in your journey toward initiation?*

3. *How have your sponsor, the RCIA team, and the parish community been a "living stone" and a "royal priest" for you?*

Quotable Quotes:

"Very truly, I tell you, the one who believes in me will also do the works that I do and, in fact, will do greater works than these because I am going to the Father."
(John 14:12)

Did You Know?

Vestments are the special garments worn by ministers at the celebration of liturgy. They originated in the time of the late Roman Empire. The ordinary clothing for men at this time was a long tunic tied at the waist (the origin of the present-day alb and cincture) and a large serape-like over-garment (the origin of the present-day chasuble). Priests wear the alb, chasuble, and stole (a narrow band of cloth worn across the back of the neck and hanging down the front) as did Roman judges and other officials as a sign of their office. Bishops also wear the same vestments but with the addition of a mitre (a pointed hat, to symbolize their office of ruling, like a crown). Deacons wear albs, dalmatics (similar to a chasuble but closed on the sides), and stoles worn over only one shoulder.

The Church Says:

In baptism, a person is consecrated priest, prophet, and king, and thus shares in the common priesthood of all believers. Thus, through the sacrament of baptism we share in the priesthood of Jesus Christ. We are called to offer spiritual sacrifices to God through Jesus Christ and are sent out to serve and to proclaim the Good News of Jesus Christ in the world.

There is yet another form of priesthood, which is called the ministerial priesthood. While the common priesthood of all believers is worked out in a life of faith, hope, and love, the ordained priesthood exists in order to assist and serve the full flowering of the baptismal call of all. The center and high point of the ministerial priesthood is the celebration of the sacraments, in particular, the celebration of the Eucharist.

For This Week:

I want to remember:

I want to put my faith into action by:

Questions to Explore:

Prayer for the Week:

Jesus, you are the cornerstone of our faith.
Like your first followers, we place our faith in
*   you, our eternal priest.*
Send your Spirit upon us
*   that we might be your chosen people,*
*   a royal priesthood.*
Help us to follow you in faith,
*   for you are the Way, the Truth,*
*   and the Life.*
Empower us each day to hear your Word
*   and heed its call to live in your marvelous*
*   light.*
Nurture us with your Word
*   that we might do your works in a hungry*
*   and hurting world.*
We ask this in your name. Amen.

Sixth Sunday of Easter

Scripture:

Acts 8:5-8, 14-17
Psalm 66:1-3, 4-5, 6-7, 16, 20
1 Peter 3:15-18
John 14:15-21

Focus:

THE SACRAMENT OF CONFIRMATION

Reflection:

Directions: *In the space provided write a letter to the Holy Spirit, asking for the gifts you desire in order to live out your love for Christ as you grow in faith and holiness, and expressing your gratitude for the abiding presence of the Spirit.*

Questions:

1. *What action-response do you expect to make to the sealing or consecration to the Holy Spirit in the sacrament of confirmation?*

2. *How does the Spirit even now strengthen your resolve to live your faith in times of struggle and misunderstanding?*

3. *In what ways has the Holy Spirit bridged the gap of prejudice among the faithful in the Church and in your own life?*

Memorable People:

The feast of saints Philip and James is celebrated on May 1. John's gospel mentions Philip several times as the one found by Jesus who responded, without hesitation, to the call to become an apostle. Today's reading from the Book of Acts tells of the success of Philip, the deacon, among the Samaritans, the splintered northern tribe of Israelites hated by the faithful Jews. These two great missionaries, one an apostle and another a deacon of the early Church, are often confused. There is reference at the close of the second century to the two daughters of St. Philip the Apostle, who recounted miracles attributed to their father, including raising a dead man to life. The apostle James became the bishop of Jerusalem and was consulted by Peter in the dispute over allowing Gentiles to become Christians without the Jewish custom of circumcision. Many came to believe through the preaching of James and he is believed to be the author of the epistle that bears his name.

Did You Know?

In Catholic Churches, the place where the sacred chrism is kept, along with the oil of catechumens and the oil of the sick, is called the ambry. It can be a prominent shelf or pedestal near the baptismal font, or a glass case in which the containers of oil are displayed and honored. Visit the Church with your sponsor or godparent and find out where the ambry is located.

The Church Says:

Confirmation is one of the three sacraments of initiation, along with baptism and Eucharist. The sign of Christ's presence is in the laying on of hands and the anointing with chrism. The anointing with holy oil or chrism at confirmation is a consecration, imparting a unique, indelible spiritual seal on the confirmed, strengthening their baptism. This perfumed oil is consecrated by the bishop on Holy Thursday at the cathedral for parish use throughout the year. This chrism or oil expresses the richness of the gifts of the Spirit poured out upon the believer in the sacrament. A prayer accompanies the laying on of the hands over the believer to ask the Spirit to strengthen the believer with seven gifts. The Holy Spirit pours out the gifts of wisdom, understanding, right judgment, courage, knowledge, reverence, and wonder and awe in the sacrament of confirmation, making us a holy people, transformed and ready to partake of the banquet of the Eucharist. From the table of the Eucharist the fully initiated are sent forth as apostles and witnesses to the ends of the earth. Thus, confirmation anoints and empowers the baptized to be a witness to Christ in the world.

For This Week:

I want to remember:

I want to put my faith into action by:

Questions to Explore:

Prayer for the Week:

*Spirit of truth, be our
source of strength
as we journey
to the sacraments of
initiation.
By the gift of God, the
risen Christ
abides with us, your
chosen people,
through you, most
Holy Spirit.
Purify us and make us
holy in your sight;
overcome our human
limitations
through your abiding
presence.
At the dawn of each new
day,
fill us with joy,
that we may be your*
*consecrated,
your holy ones.
Guide our path that we
may walk each day
in the newness of your
life.
Inspire us to share the
Good News
of Jesus dying and
rising
for all of humankind
to the ends of the
earth.
As we celebrate the joy of
the Risen Jesus,
we anticipate with hope
his return in glory at
the end of time.
Let us live with, in, and
for you,
Spirit of Jesus. Amen.*

Seventh Sunday of Easter

Scripture:

Acts 1:12-14
Psalm 27:1-4, 7-8
1 Peter 4:13-16
John 17:1-11

Focus:

CHRISTIAN UNITY

Reflection:

Directions: *Read this priestly prayer of Jesus, a portion of his farewell address to his followers, and reflect upon its meaning for you as a disciple today:*

> *After Jesus had spoken these words, he looked up to heaven and said, "Father, the hour has come; glorify your Son so that the Son may glorify you, since you have given him authority over all people, to give eternal life to all whom you have given him. And this is eternal life, that they may know you, the only true God, and Jesus Christ whom you have sent. I glorified you on earth by finishing the work that you gave me to do. So now, Father, glorify me in your own presence with the glory that I had in your presence before the world existed. I have made your name known to those whom you gave me from the world. They were yours, and you gave them to me, and they have kept your word. Now they know that everything you have given me is from you; for the words that you gave to me I have given to them, and they have received them and know in truth that I came from you; and they have believed that you sent me. I am asking on their behalf; I am not asking on behalf of the world, but on behalf of those whom you gave me, because they are yours. All mine are yours, and yours are mine; and I have been glorified in them. And now I am no longer in the world, but they are in the world, and I am coming to you. . . ." (John 17:1-11).*

Questions:

1. *What is your response to this prayer of Jesus for the first disciples and for you as a disciple today?*

2. *How can you come to "know" the one true God and thus have eternal life?*

3. *What is your hopeful expectation, as you grow deeper in your commitment to follow Jesus?*

Did You Know?

A week of prayer for Christian Unity is celebrated each year in January. It begins January 18 and concludes on January 25, the feast of the Conversion of St. Paul. The Second Vatican Council was a watershed moment in the history of the Catholic Church, representing a turning point in ecumenical relations. The ecumenical movement aims to promote the restoration of unity among all Christians. From this point onward, dialogue has continued between the Catholic Church and other Christian denominations.

The Church Says:

The Church has four characteristics or marks as proclaimed in the Nicene Creed, formulated in 381: the Church is one (unity), holy, catholic (universal), and apostolic.

This mark of unity is a truth that we believe and proclaim is a gift given by the Holy Spirit and is of the very essence of the people of God who are bound together as one in Christ. This basic union must be visible as well as spiritual, for it makes the Church what it is. Unity is a result of our redemption in Christ, which restores relationship with God and one another. Yet we experience the Christian Church divided. In our human sinfulness, the history of the Church is blotted with divisions. These divisions create scandal and diminish the Church's witness in the world. We all share in the responsibility for these divisions among believers in Christ. Therefore, we are called as a Church and as individuals to heal divisions and work for unity.

Our first responsibility is to live faithfully our own conversion and heal divisions within the Catholic community by putting our own house in order. As we develop attitudes of acceptance, tolerance, and cooperation, the need for triumphalism or denominational rivalry will have no place within the Catholic Church. The unifying power of dialogue, within theological commissions and Church bodies, takes time and patience. The long-term goal of the ecumenical movement is to gather all the work of Christ's Spirit into one Body. We are all called to pray for Christian unity.

For This Week:

I want to remember:

I want to put my faith into action by:

Questions to Explore:

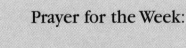

Prayer for the Week:

Almighty and eternal God,
you gather the scattered sheep
and watch over those who have scattered.

Look kindly on all who follow Jesus, your Son.
You have marked them with the seal of one
baptism,
now make them one in the fullness of faith
and unite them in the bond of love.

We ask this through Christ our Lord. Amen.
(Household Blessings and Prayers, p. 160)

Pentecost

Scripture:

Acts 2:1-11
Psalm 104:1, 24, 29-30, 31, 34
1 Corinthians 12:3-7, 12-13
John 20:19-23

Focus:

THE HOLY SPIRIT

Reflection:

Directions: *The gifts and fruits of the Holy Spirit are listed in the space below. After reading through the list, think about a situation or experience you have had in which the Holy Spirit sustained or surprised you. Describe this experience in the space provided. Then check off the gifts and fruits of the Spirit you identified at this time.*

MY EXPERIENCE OF BEING SUSTAINED OR SURPRISED BY THE HOLY SPIRIT

THE FRUITS OF THE SPIRIT (Galatians 5:22)

love	kindness
joy	goodness
peace	faithfulness
patience	gentleness
self-control	

THE GIFTS OF THE HOLY SPIRIT

wisdom	knowledge
understanding	piety
counsel	wonder and awe
fortitude	(fear of the Lord)

Questions:

1. *The Holy Spirit is given not only to individuals, but to the Church. What are some gifts and fruits of the Spirit that you observe in the Church?*

2. *How have you experienced being sent forth to spread the Good News to others?*

3. *What gift or fruit of the Holy Spirit do you seek in order to be a reconciler at home, in the workplace, and/or in your faith community?*

Quotable Quotes:

Twelfth-century abbess, Hildegard of Bingen, thought to be a mystic, wrote the following Antiphon for the Holy Spirit: *The spirit of God is a life that bestows life, root of the world tree and wind in its boughs. Scrubbing out sins, she rubs oil into wounds. She is glistening life, alluring all praise, all-awakening, all-resurrecting.* (Source: *Symphonia*, translated and edited by Barbara Newman, Ithaca: Cornell University Press, 1988, p. 141.)

Did You Know?

St. Gereon, the oldest church in Cologne, Germany, is named after a fourth-century Roman soldier martyred for the faith. The church was destroyed in the fire-bombing of World War II and rebuilt in 1979. The reconstructed dome of the amazing, ten-sided Roman tower in the main body of the church rivals that of St. Sophia in Istanbul. The ceiling of the dome is painted a deep red background against which stand out golden "Easter drops." The onlooker perceives in this rebuilt church the fire of the Spirit reanimating a people rising from the evils of Nazism, war, and the total bombing of the city.

The Church Says:

The feast of Pentecost celebrates the outpouring of the Spirit on the disciples. It is the birthday of the Church.

The Holy Spirit, the third person of the Trinity, who is worshiped and glorified, has acted throughout history. The Spirit was present at the time of creation as the wind hovered over the waters of chaos, and as God breathed life into the clay of the ground, forming a human person. The Spirit spoke through the prophets. The Spirit overshadowed Mary and brought about the incarnation. Jesus came to bring forth God's reign. With his death, resurrection, and ascension, the continuation of this mission is handed over to the Church, empowered by the constant presence of the Spirit. All believers are baptized as messengers of this Good News to the world.

The Spirit makes us strong, loving, and wise (2 Timothy 1:7), bidding us to make bold proclamation as did the apostles on that first Pentecost. The Spirit bestows gifts upon the People of God to bring about God's reign in the world. The Spirit propels us beyond human limitations through new life and energy. The Spirit does amazing things through us that are surprising and unpredictable. The Spirit challenges our comfortable existence as we are transformed to live in God's freedom, strength, and power. Those who have eyes to see recognize the continual activity of the Spirit.

For This Week:

I want to remember:

I want to put my faith into action by:

Questions to Explore:

Prayer for the Week:

Come, Holy Spirit, come!
And from your celestial home
Shed a ray of light divine!
Come, Father of the poor!
Come, source of all our store!
Come, within our bosoms shine!
You, of comforters the best;
You, the soul's most welcome guest;
Sweet refreshment here below;
In our labor, rest most sweet;
Grateful coolness in the heat;
Solace in the midst of woe.
O most blessed Light divine,
Shine within these hearts of yours,
And our inmost being fill!
Where you are not, [we have] naught,
Nothing good in deed or thought,

Nothing free from taint
of ill.
Heal our wounds, our strength
renew;
On our dryness pour your dew;
Wash the stains of guilt away:
Bend the stubborn heart and will;
Melt the frozen, warm the chill;
Guide the steps that go astray.
On the faithful, who adore
And confess you, evermore
In your sev'nfold gift descend;
Give them virtue's sure reward;
Give them your salvation, Lord;
Give them joys that never end.
Amen. Alleluia.

ORDINARY TIME

Second Sunday in Ordinary Time

Scripture:

Isaiah 49:3, 5-6
Psalm 40:2, 4, 7-8, 8-9, 10
1 Corinthians 1:1-3
John 1:29-34

Focus:

NAMES OF JESUS

Reflection:

Directions: *After these titles for Jesus, write your insights and thoughts as to their meaning for your life.*

Lord

Christ

Son of God

Son of Man

Questions:

1. *What name for Jesus do you find most significant? Why?*

2. *What does this name reveal to you about Jesus and his mission?*

Memorable People:

Luis de Leon was an Augustinian monk and professor who lived in late sixteenth-century Spain (d. 1591). His family background (Jews forcibly converted) along with his criticism of the Latin translation of the Bible drew the attention of the Inquisition and he spent some time in prison. He was a gifted translator (Hebrew, Latin, and Greek) and is most noted for his prose work "On the Names of Christ" (*Divine Inspiration: The Life of Jesus in World Poetry*, Robert Atawan, George Dardess, Peggy Rosenthan, editors, Oxford University Press, New York, 1998, p. 566).

Did You Know?

The Litany of the Holy Name contains some forty different titles for Jesus. A sampling of those titles are: "dawn of justice, prince of peace, pattern of patience, model of obedience, seeker of souls, refuge, courage of martyrs and crown of saints." The entire litany can be found in many prayer books and in the *Catholic Household Blessings & Prayers*.

The Church Says:

In confessing Jesus as the Savior, the New Testament writers not only used contemporary cultural images to describe his unique significance, they also reached back into the rich heritage of Hebrew scripture and used Old Testament titles and designations to illuminate his identity. The Christian community continued to explore the profound mystery of Jesus in the immediate post-biblical times, and especially in the christological discussions held at the councils of Nicea (325), Constantinople (381), and Chalcedon (451). "Christology" is the term used by the Church to delineate attempts to plumb the mystery of Jesus' identity, a task that continues today.

In today's gospel text, John the Baptist, pointing out Jesus, refers to him as "Lamb of God" and "God's Chosen One." These scriptural titles, and other adopted titles of Jesus from the Old Testament (such as those in today's first reading—"servant" and "light to the nations") express belief in Jesus' unique identity. The fourth gospel also employs other descriptions for Jesus: "eternal Word" (*logos*); "light of the world"; "the way, truth, and life"; "bread of life"; "living water"; "good shepherd"; "sheep gate"; and "vine." But among all the titles bestowed on Jesus in the New Testament, four stand out: "Lord," "Christ," "Son of God," and "Son of Man."

The title "Lord" is used to connote honor, as well as to indicate the second coming of the one who is now exalted by God and will usher in the end times. This name for Jesus indicates the sense of Jesus' oneness with the divine nature of God. The title "Christ" literally means anointed. It describes Jesus' status as the promised one of God, the Savior, whose messianic mission is uniquely that of priest, prophet, and king. The unique relationship of Jesus as God's own Son is used to indicate that he shares in the divine nature. Jesus uses the title "Son of Man" himself to describe his mission, his suffering and death, and his return at the end of time. God the Father in the resurrection vindicates the crucified Jesus who came to serve and give his life as ransom for many.

For This Week:

I want to remember:

I want to put my faith into action by:

Questions to Explore:

Prayer for the Week:

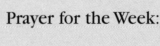

Jesus, you are the Christ . . .
Jesus, you are Lord . . .
Jesus, you are the Messiah . . .
Jesus, you are Son of God and Son of Man . . .
Jesus, you are the light to the nations . . .
Jesus, you are the chosen one of God . . .
Jesus, you are the servant of God . . .
Jesus, you are the eternal Word . . .
Jesus, you are the light of the world . . .
Jesus you are the way, the truth, and the life . . .
Jesus, you are the bread of life . . .
Jesus, you are the good shepherd . . .

Third Sunday in Ordinary Time

Scripture:

Isaiah 8:23–9:3
Psalm 27:1, 4, 13-14
1 Corinthians 1:10-14, 17
Matthew 4:12-23

Focus:

VOCATION

Reflection:

Directions: Next to the description of a typical day in the ministry of Jesus, write about your vocation/call as you carry on his mission to today's world:

He calls his disciples to abandon everything and follow him

travels throughout the region of Galilee

teaches in their synagogues

proclaims the Good News—God's kingdom is at hand

cures people of illness and disease

Questions:

1. *How have you responded to this call in very ordinary ways?*

2. *Who proclaimed the Good News to you?*

3. *What does it mean for you to be in union with others in the Catholic community?*

Memorable People:

The saint popularly known as the Little Flower is St. Therese of Lisieux. As a young nun she was told to write the autobiography of her life. While reluctant, Therese obeyed her superior, focusing not on the events of her difficult life, but on the grace that God freely showered on her. Therese is a woman of strength who endured excruciating spiritual darkness and the wracking physical illness of tuberculosis. Yet she continually rejoiced in the outpouring of divine love for her. Her short life is a witness of how the most ordinary human existence contains material for extraordinary holiness. She encourages all believers to follow her "little way," which she describes as an attitude of unlimited hope in God's merciful love.

The Church Says:

Another word for "call," which is commonly used in the Catholic community, is "vocation." All people are called by God to share divine life and eternal happiness with God. Through the salvation won for all, Jesus has transformed us in the Holy Spirit as adopted children of God and heirs to God's kingdom. In response to this intimate relationship with God, the baptized are called to further the mission of Jesus in the world. The mission of Jesus is the mission, not only of ordained and vowed priests, deacons, brothers, and sisters, but of all the baptized. Thus, the vocation or "call" of all believers is rooted in baptism.

Pope John Paul II uses the image of the vine and the branches to portray this relationship. As members of the Church, we are in union with Christ and therefore with one another. All people for all times are thus bound together in love. It is love that compels us to follow and imitate Jesus. We have been gifted, that is, graced, by God. These unique gifts and graces freely given to us by God are to be used to build up the community of believers. When we proclaim the Good News of Jesus' death and resurrection in our living and through our actions, we continue Jesus' mission in the world.

Like Jesus' call of his apostles, our call comes in the ordinariness of daily living. It comes as a light that gives us the wisdom to see the Good News of Jesus dying and rising with us, raising us out of darkness and death. As this Christian vocation flowers and bears fruit, we proclaim the Good News in word and in action. The holiness of our lives brings the light of the Good News to those we meet in the course of our ordinary lives.

For This Week:

I want to remember:

I want to put my faith into action by:

Questions to Explore:

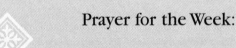

Prayer for the Week:

God of light, you lift us out of the darkness of sin
and the gloom of our fears
by sending your Son Jesus to die and rise for us.
We proclaim the Good News
that Jesus dies with us each time we die
through failure, suffering, or despair.
Through the power of his marvelous resurrection,
he gathers us and lifts us up
out of the trials of this life
and we are renewed and re-formed.
We are a graced and gifted people,
called to share our dyings and risings with others,
that they may come to believe
in the resurrection and the life.
Strengthen us to live in holiness
that we might bring your wonderful light
into our world.
Give us the courage to share our stories,
our Good News with those who seek the light.
Abide with us as we journey in faith,
anticipating the fountain of living waters
and the table of living bread. Amen.

Fourth Sunday in Ordinary Time

Scripture:

Zephaniah 2:3, 3:12-13
Psalm 146:6-7, 8-9, 9-10
1 Corinthians 1:26-31
Matthew 5:1-2

Focus:

FOUNDATIONS OF CHRISTIAN MORALITY

Reflection:

Directions: *Below are the statements contained in the Beatitudes. Imagine that Jesus is saying each of these Beatitudes to you. Which of the Beatitudes addresses the issues you face in your life right now? Do you find comfort in what Jesus is saying? How do these Beatitudes encourage you to change your actions?*

Blest are the poor in spirit
Blest are the sorrowing
Blest are the lowly
Blest are they who hunger and thirst for holiness
Blest are they who show mercy
Blest are the single-hearted
Blest are the peacemakers
Blest are those persecuted for holiness' sake
Blest are you when you are insulted and persecuted because of me

Questions:

1. *Select one of the Beatitudes and indicate how it can be a guide to identifying right moral choices.*

2. *Select another Beatitude and indicate how it might affect your attitudes and actions.*

3. *Select a third Beatitude and write a prayer asking God to nurture this attitude in your daily life.*

Quotable Quotes:

St. Leo the Great preached, "Christian, recognize your dignity and, now that you share in God's own nature, do not return to your former base condition by sinning. Remember who is your head and of whose body you are a member. Never forget that you have been rescued from the power of darkness and brought into the light of the kingdom of God" (*Sermo* 21 in nat. Dom., *3*: PL 54, 192C).

Memorable People:

Saint Elizabeth Ann Seton (1774-1821), born in the United States, was a wife and mother. When her husband died, she continued to care for her children, even after she established a religious order, the American Sisters of Charity. Her prayer expresses the desire to walk along the paths of right, in spite of our human weakness: "Almighty and Giver of all mercies, Father of all, who knows my heart and pities its weaknesses, you know the desire of my soul to do your will. It struggles to wing its flight to you its creator and sinks again in sorrow for that imperfection which draws it back to earth. How long will I contend with sin and morality. . . . Redeemer of sinners! Who gave your life to save us, assist a miserable sinner who strives with the corruption and desires above all things to break the snares of the enemy" (Woodeene Koenig-Bricker, Prayers of the Saints, Harper SanFransisco, 1996, pp. 33-4).

The Church Says:

The "natural law" is knowable by all people, not just the Christian faithful. Indeed, the exercise of one's reason opens the human person to the ways of God. Since the natural law is knowable, the question for theologians is whether there is a specific Christian morality. The answer is yes, because its motivation and impetus lies in pleasing and loving God. Created, redeemed, and sanctified by God in Christ, the believer may very well say and do the same things as nonbelievers, but from a different perspective—which makes all the difference.

How is the moral person formed? Morally responsible Christians are formed by baptism and a whole set of experiences, values, and symbols that shape conscience and, indeed, consciousness. It is not reason alone that forms a Christian conscience. The whole human person—a mysterious complex of emotions, understandings, and sensibilities, transformed by Christ—takes part in the moral life. Indeed, Catholicism forms a certain kind of character. The community itself has a vital role to play in this character formation because of the witness it hands on regarding Jesus. This witness is a powerful message about "creation, liberation, covenant, incarnation, death, and resurrection" (NDictTheol 684).

Every believer bears the responsibility of informing his or her own conscience in order to act rightly and justly in the world. Good preaching, sound religious education, an understanding of scripture, spiritual direction, the witness and example of other Christians, and the authoritative teaching of the Church help to form one's conscience. This formation is a lifelong process wherein the believer sifts through experience and with the grace of the Holy Spirit pursues the path of right (CCC 1785).

For This Week:

I want to remember:

I want to put my faith into action by:

Questions to Explore:

Prayer for the Week:

Blessed are you, Lord our God,
*   for calling us into your kingdom.*
Blessed are we to know your ways in our hearts.
We are grateful to be counted among
*   those whom you call blessed.*
We desire to be poor in spirit in order to be
*   filled with you.*
Teach our hearts your ways
*   for you alone can satisfy our hunger and*
*   emptiness.*
Give me a courageous heart to be undaunted
*   by words and actions that bring hurt to my*
*   soul.*
Open us to extend your comfort
*   and compassion to others.*
We give thanks to you our God, for all the ways
*   you invite me to abide in you. Amen.*

Fifth Sunday in Ordinary Time

Scripture:

Isaiah 58:7-10
Psalm 112:4-5, 6-7, 8-9
1 Corinthians 2:1-5
Matthew 5:13-16

Focus:

THE SOCIAL TEACHING OF THE CHURCH: PREFERENTIAL OPTION FOR THE POOR

Reflection:

Directions: *In the space provided, write about your recollection of an encounter with the poor, oppressed, or homeless. Clearly indicate your feelings and responses.*

Questions:

1. *Briefly describe the printed accounts you selected by answering the following: What group(s) are addressed? What is the issue? How are the poor, homeless, oppressed, or marginalized presented?*

2. *What might your perception of the issue be if you place yourself in their situation?*

3. *What would alleviate the cause of this injustice?*

4. *How would you want others to respond to you if you were in a similar situation?*

Did You Know?

The Corporal Works of Mercy are:

Feed the hungry	Clothe the naked	Visit the imprisoned
Give drink to the thirsty	Shelter the homeless	Bury the dead
	Visit the sick	

FOR YOUR INFORMATION: Numerous Catholic parishes engage in activities to alleviate the plight of the poor and oppressed. Soup kitchens, food pantries, and shelters for the homeless or victims of domestic violence are examples of some of these activities. Many churches open their doors in winter in order to shelter the homeless.

The Campaign for Human Development was established by the Church to collect money for programs of education and self-help that specifically address the root causes of poverty and oppression.

The Church Says:

The Church has always been concerned with the problems and potentials of human society. The modern era of rapid growth and expansion has caused Church leaders to develop a more detailed social teaching. Key to this current teaching is the preferential option for the poor. This means that the Church is committed to the poor and exhorts all believers to commit themselves to assist all those in society who are marginalized and oppressed. Thus, in making moral decisions, the needs and concerns of the poor are to be given priority over other issues. This option for the poor includes all those who are exploited or robbed of their basic human dignity.

This option for the poor arises out of the experience of the God who liberated the chosen people from slavery in Egypt and who continued to call that same people through the prophets to alleviate the suffering of the poor. Jesus sums up the Old Testament promises and challenges of this liberation in his life, death, and mission to the poor. Through baptism all believers share in the mission of Jesus the liberator. In the Second Vatican Council, the bishops of the world asserted that the laity work toward universal progress in liberation. The notion of liberation was further developed and enlarged by the Medellin and Puebla conferences of South American bishops who spoke of the Church as being allied with the poor.

For This Week:

I want to remember:

I want to put my faith into action by:

Questions to Explore:

Prayer for the Week:

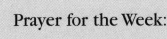

Jesus, you showed us the way to live.
You always had time for the poor, the sick,
the outcasts.
You fed the hungry.
Through the example of your encounters with
the poor,
we can discover how to be salt for the earth
and the light for the world.
Give us the courage to act in the face of
opposition and ridicule.
Give us the willingness to reach out
and embrace our brothers and sisters
who are the unwilling victims of injustices.
Keep us faithful to this commitment
even when we are challenged or ridiculed.
We ask this in your name. Amen.

Sixth Sunday in Ordinary Time

Scripture:

Sirach 15:15-20
Psalm 119:1-2, 4-5, 17-18, 33-34
1 Corinthians 2:6-10
Matthew 5:17-37

Focus:

HUMAN FREEDOM AND CHRIST'S LAW OF LOVE

Reflection:

Directions: *Look at the continuum below. Place yourself on this continuum by putting an x on the line, indicating how you responded to God's laws one year ago, and another x on the line to signify how you respond now. Underneath the line write concrete examples of this change.*

Disobeying   Obeying God's laws   Responding
God's laws   out of duty   out of love

Questions:

1. *What are the occasions, issues, situations, or people that cause you to choose your way over God's wise commands?*

2. *What laws of God are the most difficult for you to keep?*

Memorable People:

Saint Thomas More (1478-1535) was born in London, educated at Oxford, earned a law degree, and was elected to Parliament. He became Lord Chancellor of England. Three years later he resigned his position because of his opposition to the king's divorce. Refusing to take the Oath of Succession, he was sent to the Tower of London and was tried. His defense of his faith led to his beheading in 1535. The stage play and movie *A Man for All Seasons* details the last years of his life with his unflinching conviction to live up to his faith in the face of the king's wrath and his eventual martyrdom. St. Thomas More, whose feast day is June 22, is the patron saint of lawyers.

Did You Know?

The word "commandment" comes from words that mean "joining hands with" another. Living according to God's commandments unites us with God. God and we live life together with common values. The word "obey" literally means *to listen intently*. Thus, when we obey God's commandments we listen intently in our hearts to hear God's Word so that we are able to join our hands with God's as we live.

The Church Says:

All people are born with free will, the ability to choose right or wrong. From the time of Adam and Eve, people have made choices for evil as well as for good. People greatly value freedom. Yet freedom carries with it the possibility of choosing evil. God gave Moses the Ten Commandments. Faithful living of these commandments was a sign of the relationship between God and God's people. Over time, the Jewish people came to observe 613 prescriptions. The scribes and Pharisees of Jesus' time dedicated themselves to following these laws. Jesus, through how he lived and taught, brought us to a deeper understanding of what the law is about. Rather than stating we must follow the law and do no wrong, he called us to go the next step and make choices based on love. The new commandment of love Jesus gave is etched on the hearts of believers. Christians are invited to an attitude of love, which permeates their entire being and is lived out in specific situations.

Christian believers can fail to live up to God's law through legalism, observing the letter of the law to the detriment of the spirit of the law. On the other extreme, failure to live up to God's law occurs through over-emphasizing the spirit of the law and failing to carry out its specific aims. Christians do not fulfill the commandment of love only out of a sense of duty. Rather, God's love for each of us evokes a response of love. Christians desire to live in faithfulness to their relationship to God in Christ. Love is the sign that marks the true disciple of Christ.

For This Week:

I want to remember:

I want to put my faith into action by:

Questions to Explore:

Prayer for the Week:

God of love,
*   you create me out of love.*
You desire only my love in return.
Etch your love ever more deeply in my heart.
When I am faced with choices,
*   make your way known to me.*
I pray that the way of love
*   be as attractive to me*
*   and as sweet as honey.*
Truly teach me your wisdom and way.
Amen.

Seventh Sunday in Ordinary Time

Scripture:

Leviticus 19:1-2, 17-18
Psalm 103:1-2, 3-4, 8, 10, 12-13
1 Corinthians 3:16-23
Matthew 5:38-48

Focus:

UNIVERSAL CALL TO HOLINESS

Reflection:

PART I

Directions: *In this week's gospel, Jesus calls us to love even our enemies. Reflect back over your life. Who are the people who in some way have been an enemy to you? What would you have to do or to let go of in order to love them? Write your thoughts below.*

PART II

Directions: *This gospel also states that we are to be perfect as God is perfect. Make two columns. In one column, list all the attitudes you think Jesus might include in being perfect, whole, or holy. In the second, list behaviors which you think Jesus might consider whole or perfect. Then consider whether these attitudes and behaviors seem possible for you to live.*

Attitudes   Behaviors

Quotable Quotes:

"*There are two ways, one of life and one of death:
and great is the difference between the two ways.
The way of life is this: first, you shall love God, who created you;
second, your neighbor as yourself.*"
(Didache 1:1)

Did You Know?

The Church document, "Justice in the World" (November 30, 1971), is the first on social teaching to derive from a synod of bishops. One of its great contributions is the linking of the gospel message of loving one's neighbor to the pursuit of justice. The mission of the Church, and thus of individual members, is not only a striving toward a spiritual wholeness and holiness, but working in the world for a holiness of right relationships.

The Church Says:

All people are called to holiness. Over the centuries before the Second Vatican Council, 1962-1965, the Church emphasized the call to holiness that belongs to priests and women and men in religious life. In a rather radical reorientation which goes back to the New Testament and the understanding of the early Church, the Council taught that *all* people are called to holiness by reason of their baptism. This means that married couples, parents, single persons, the poor, sick, and all the baptized are called to holiness. They express God's love in their particular way and situation.

To grow in holiness we need the strength and support of the Christian community. Prayer, participation in the sacraments, ascetical practices, looking to Mary and the witness of the saints as examples are all helps in living a life of holiness, the call of love.

The call to holiness is given as a gift from God. Yet this call requires a response in action. Making moral choices, living the commandments, loving our enemies, and practicing the Beatitudes are ways of cooperating with God's grace and call to holiness. In cooperating with God's grace through actions, believers are united with Christ and with the entire Trinity.

For This Week:

I want to remember:

I want to put my faith into action by:

Questions to Explore:

Prayer for the Week:

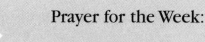
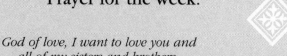

God of love, I want to love you and
*   all of my sisters and brothers.*
Yet, at times, I get hurt
*   or I see real harm that is done*
*   and I find it hard to love.*
Help me when love is beyond my under-
*   standing.*
Give me your eyes
*   to see as you see those persons,*
*   who feel like enemies to me.*
Give me your grace to love myself as well.
Teach me to treat my body well,
*   since my body is your temple.*
Let your love wash over me and over all of
*   your people*
*   just as your sun shines on all. Amen.*

Eighth Sunday in Ordinary Time

Scripture:

Isaiah 49:14-15
Psalm 62:2-3, 6-7, 8-9
1 Corinthians 4:1-5
Matthew 6:24-34

Focus:

DIVINE PROVIDENCE

Reflection:

Directions: *Reflect upon these teachings of Jesus, taken from the scriptures. When you have finished reflecting, use the space below to write your own prayer of surrender to the loving care of God. In your prayer name those things that have taken precedence over God. Ask God to strengthen your faith in God's providence, and your hope in God's steadfast love and charity, that you might carry God's love in you to others in need.*

You cannot give yourself to God and money.
Life is more than food, the body more valuable than clothes.
You are more important than the birds, the grass, and the flowers.
O, weak in faith, stop worrying.
God knows all that you need.
Seek first God's kingship over you.
Seek God's way of holiness.
Let tomorrow take care of itself. Today has troubles enough of its own.

Prayer of Surrender

Questions:

1. *How would you explain God's providential care to a friend who is stressed and worried?*

2. *In what ways have you experienced God's care in times of trouble?*

3. *What evidence of God's bringing all of creation to fullness and perfection can you name?*

Quotable Quotes:

"And can any of you by worrying add a single hour to your span of life? . . .
But if God so clothes the grass of the field, which is alive today and tomorrow
is thrown into the oven, will he not much more clothe you . . . ?" (Matthew 6:27-30)

Memorable People:

Julian of Norwich, a mystic and spiritual teacher, lived in solitude in fourteenth-century England. Her spiritual writings flowed out of her visions—her encounters with God. Her spiritual insight into the feminine side of God presents a spirituality relevant for many contemporary seekers as well as for people of her own time. Among the many truths she offers to modern readers, Julian offers this comfort: "God does not promise that we will not be troubled or distressed. God, instead, assures us that we will not be overcome."

The Church Says:

Divine providence refers to the Church's teaching that God not only creates, but also guides all of creation to fullness and perfection throughout the course of human history. This teaching is at the core of the sacred scriptures; the Old Testament is based upon the covenant between God and Israel and the New Testament reveals the fulfillment of this covenant-salvation through the ministry, death, and resurrection of Jesus. Jesus came to reveal the love and care of God, who answers our prayers, forgives our sins, and invites us to eternal life.

Humankind is free to share in God's providence by collaborating with God's plan in completing the work of creation—bringing all things to fullness and perfection. Evil, that is, working against God's plan, is the option open to those who deliberately choose to turn their backs on God. Illness, human limitations, and tragedies are part of the human condition, through no fault of our own. Yet we believe that God can and does work through all things to the good for those who love God. Only through the eyes of faith can the believer begin to comprehend the mystery of divine providence, human freedom, and the problem of evil.

For This Week:

I want to remember:

I want to put my faith into action by:

Questions to Explore:

Prayer for the Week:

Almighty and ever-present God,
your watchful care reaches across
the expanse of the universe.
Who am I that you should care for me?
I am a speck of little significance
in the vastness of the cosmos.
Yet your love for me is like that
of a mother for her infant.
Your love goes far beyond
the capacity of human love
for you constantly reassure me
that you will never forget,
that you will never abandon me.
I surrender my life, my concerns,
and my struggles
to trust in your unfathomable love.
Take and receive me
into your loving embrace. Amen.

Ninth Sunday in Ordinary Time

Scripture:

Deuteronomy 11:18, 26-28, 32
Psalm 31:2-3, 3-4, 17, 25
Romans 3:21-25, 28
Matthew 7:21-27

Focus:

JUSTIFICATION

Reflection:

Part I

Directions: *In today's scripture readings you heard, "Be hearers and doers of the Word." What do you understand by that phrase? Describe a time when you have witnessed someone being a doer of the spoken Word.*

Part II

Directions: *In light of the gospel, describe in what way the person is building a house on rock and then retell the story from the perspective of a house built on sand.*

A. Joe and Sally live quietly in their small home. They both work in a local factory. Their children attend the public school. As in any community, there are the poor, the homeless, and the hungry. Joe, Sally, and the family spend one Saturday a month at the local food pantry bagging groceries. When asked why they do it, they simply reply that it's the least they can do to help others.

B. Lorenzo heads the personnel department of a large corporation. He's very active in the Big Brother, Big Sister movement in his community. Some of his family and friends ridicule his involvement saying that he's just an easy target. Lorenzo remains faithful to his involvement and encourages others from his corporation to get involved. He believes that his dedication makes a difference in the community.

Marie, a widow, has been retired for many years. She lives in an apartment on her fixed income. Whenever anyone in the complex needs a ride or help with child care, Marie is always the first person they ask. She helps whenever and however she can.

How do you describe the gift of God's grace?

How do you respond to the gift of grace?

Did You Know?

The Council of Trent (which held various sessions between 1546-53 A.D.) met to discuss the Protestant reformers' teaching which emphasized the universality of sin, the absolute gratuity of justification, and insisted that human freedom was destroyed by original sin. The Council of Trent proclaimed that it is possible for humans to exercise their free will and cooperate with God's grace to be renewed inwardly.

Unfortunately, these discussions at the time of the Reformation were tritely summarized as Protestants saying "faith alone" and Catholics saying "works alone" will bring about justification.

Today, Protestants and Catholics are much closer on the issue of justification because it is untenable to simply say "faith alone" or "works alone." The two, faith and works, go together.

The Church Says:

The Catholic Church teaches that justification is the action of God's grace through the salvation achieved by Jesus Christ and individuals appropriate that justification by their faith-in-action.

The central lynchpin of the doctrine of justification is Jesus and his life, death, and resurrection. Through the Holy Spirit we are joined to Christ's suffering and death when we die to sin. In the same way, we are joined to Christ's resurrection when we are born again to eternal life in baptism. Conversion is characterized as the first work of the grace given by the Holy Spirit.

The believer cannot embrace the message of salvation without also putting that Word into practice. Another approach to characterize justification is to describe it as the ground of cooperation between God's gift of grace and our human freedom. God holds out for us the possibility of conversion and believers accept this gift in faith. Individuals can choose to either accept or reject the grace of God. We need God's loving grace extended to us in order to enter into new life.

Through God's grace, a free and generous act of God, believers are justified, that is, put into right relationship with the divine.

For This Week:

I want to remember:

I want to put my faith into action by:

Questions to Explore:

Prayer for the Week:

Lord, in you I take refuge;
do not put me to shame.
Rescue me, listen to me,
hurry to save me.

Lord, in you I take refuge;
you are a rock to keep me safe.
You guide and direct me.

Lord, in you I take refuge;
help me to take courage,
to be strong,
to be brave.
You are the rock to keep me safe.
Psalm 31 (paraphrased)

Tenth Sunday in Ordinary Time

Scripture:

Hosea 6:3-6
Psalm 50:1, 8, 12-13, 14-15
Romans 4:18-25
Matthew 9:9-13

Focus:

GRACE

Reflection:

Directions: *Jesus offered the free gift of grace to Matthew, who readily responded. Jesus ate at Matthew's house with the tax collectors and sinners. The Pharisees who knew and kept the law were self-righteous and critical of Jesus for eating with tax collectors and sinners who disregard the law. Complete the following sentences with as many responses as occur to you.*

A. *I am self-righteous when . . .*

B. *I experience my own weaknesses and sinfulness, marveling in Jesus' unconditional love, when . . .*

Questions:

1. *What are some moments of grace in your journey of faith?*

2. *How would you describe God's grace in your life?*

3. *For what grace do you wish to thank God at this time in your life?*

Quotable Quotes:

The early Christians prayed, *"Let grace come and let this world pass away."*
(Didache 10:6)

Did You Know?

The cornucopia, a symbol deriving from pagan times and associated with the goddess Ceres, depicts the "horn of plenty" overflowing with flowers, fruit, and corn. In Christian art the cornucopia symbolizes the bountiful and abundant grace given by God in Jesus and overflowing through the power of the Spirit to make of us a new creation.

The Church Says:

"Grace," in Latin *gratia*, meaning thanks or favor, is the self-gift of God's life within us. Through grace we share in the intimate love of the Trinity. Because of grace we are able to call God our "Father" and Jesus our "brother." Grace is a free gift of God and is never the result of any human accomplishment.

Over the course of history the Church has struggled to identify the relationship between grace and good works. Since the time of St. Augustine (d. 430) the Church has held that the good we do is through, with, and in Christ, rather than from our own power.

The Church identifies three types of grace. Sanctifying grace is an ongoing, habitual gift that makes us who we are in accordance with God's love. It is supernatural or beyond human nature. Actual grace is given to us as a special help at particular times or for special acts. By participating in the sacraments we encounter God's gift of life, that is, the grace proper to that sacrament.

Four aspects of grace characterize the Catholic understanding of grace. Grace is experienced in the present and will be brought to fulfillment at the end of time. Grace is universally offered to all. Grace changes us and transforms us into the living body of Christ. Grace opens up the way for our communion with God.

For This Week:

I want to remember:

I want to put my faith into action by:

Questions to Explore:

Prayer for the Week:

Gracious God, you are full of gifts.
You come into my life in surprising ways.
You overflow with love
in ways that delight my soul.
You are always taking the initiative,
inviting me to your choicest banquet.
Make my heart attentive to the gifts you offer.
Draw me ever more into your love,
for it is only in you
that my soul is satisfied.
Amen.

Eleventh Sunday in Ordinary Time

Scripture:

Exodus 19:2-6
Psalm 100:1-2, 3, 5
Romans 5:6-11
Matthew 9:36–10:8

Focus:

THE MYSTERY
OF THE CHURCH

Reflection Questions:

Directions: *Jesus' ministry included teaching and healing. Jesus sends his disciples and us as our mission to continue his ministry. In the light of our participation in Jesus' ministry, respond to the following questions with as many examples as possible:*

A. *What are some ways you experience being part of the mission of Jesus?*

B. *In what ways do you help to bring about the reign of God?*

C. *The Church is . . .*

Quotable Quotes:

In dedicating a new church building for worship, St. Augustine (d. 430) preached: "This is our house of prayer, but we too are a house of God. . . . What was done when this church was being built is similar to what is done when believers are built up into Christ. When they first come to believe they are like timber and stone taken from woods and mountains. In their instruction, baptism and formation they are, so to speak, shaped, leveled and smoothed by the hands of carpenters and craftsmen. But Christians do not make a house of God until they are one in charity. . . . The work we see complete in this building is physical; it should find its spiritual counterpart in your hearts. . . . Your lives should reveal the handiwork of God's grace" (Sermon 336,1.6: PL 38, 1471-72. 1475 found in LitHrs, vol. 4, pp.1607-08).

Did You Know?

At the time of the early Christians, the word "Church," from *ecclesia,* referred only to the people, the assembly. The building where the people gathered was termed *domus,* or "house" of the Church.

The very shape of the Catholic Church buildings indicates the mystery of the Church in its gathered assembly. Some buildings are made in the shape of a cross to remind people of the loving sacrifice of Jesus Christ, the cornerstone of the Church. Some are eight-sided to emphasize the "eighth day" of creation (that is, the eternal "day" of new life with God that never ends). Other buildings are round, symbolizing universality.

The Church Says:

The Second Vatican Council defines the Church as the *People of God*, who are constituted in Christ through the Holy Spirit. The Church is both a visible reality, an organized society that exists in our world and history, and a timeless spiritual reality that transcends this world and time.

The Church is a mystery, a sacrament, that is, a sign and instrument of a deeper reality. The Church as a sacrament both contains within itself and communicates the grace of God. The Church's goal is to make holy the members of Christ's body through the gift of love given by its spouse, Jesus Christ. The Church continues the mission of Christ to bring about God's reign in this world.

The Second Vatican Council uses five images to describe the Church. The Church is a *sheepfold* or gateway to Christ. It is a cultivated *field* or *vineyard* with Christ as the vine and people as the branches. The Church is a *building of God* whose foundation and cornerstone is Jesus Christ. The Church is also the *New Jerusalem* described in the book of Revelation. And, finally, the Church is *our mother*, the spotless spouse of the spotless Lamb of God, Christ, who sacrificed himself that we might be made holy.

For This Week:

I want to remember:

I want to put my faith into action by:

Questions to Explore:

Prayer for the Week:

God of the covenant,
you have made us your holy people,
a kingdom of priests,
a holy nation.
You care for us tenderly as a shepherd.
You speak, letting us hear your voice
so that we may know the way to you.
Make our ears attentive to your calling.
Make our hearts responsive to your word.
Make our lives offerings of true worship
to give you honor and praise,
love and gratitude,
now and forever.
Amen.

Twelfth Sunday in Ordinary Time

Scripture:

Jeremiah 20:10-13
Psalm 69:8-10, 14, 17, 33-35
Romans 5:12-15
Matthew 10:26-33

Focus:

PERSECUTION AND SUFFERING

Reflection:

Directions: *Recall an experience you have had that was the cause of great mental, physical, or spiritual suffering and/or persecution (or rejection). In the space below, briefly recount the circumstances. Spend time journaling about (1) how you got through the difficulty, (2) what you learned, (3) your process of growth, and (4) your relationship with God during this period.*

Questions:

1. *How would you explain the suffering and persecution caused by natural occurrences and those caused by human sin and weakness?*

2. *What role does the community of believers have on us as we place our trust in God during difficult times?*

3. *After reflecting upon these scriptures, how will your prayer change during times of suffering and persecution?*

Quotable Quotes:

"But even the hairs of your head are all counted.
Do not be afraid; . . ." (Luke 12:7)

Did You Know?

The traditional color for Mass vestments on a martyr's feast day is red, denoting blood shed for the sake of the faith. Red is also the liturgical color signifying the Holy Spirit. There is, thus, a double meaning in the use of red on martyrs' feast days, for it is only in the Holy Spirit that the martyr could endure the pain of suffering.

The Church Says:

The human experience includes suffering in all its forms. The human pain of chronic illness, the emotional pain of grief, and the spiritual pain of desolation are all within the range of our daily existence. God does not cause suffering and pain. Suffering can be the result of natural or worldly processes or caused by the misuse of free will. We are sometimes the cause of human suffering and sometimes its recipients. When we turn our backs on God and choose evil, we begin the ripple effect of suffering. Yet we profess faith in a God of mercy who forgives us when we fail to choose the good. We believe that Jesus plunged into our human experience and endured what we endure—suffering, persecution, and death. Our wounds are the pathway of our salvation. Our sufferings lead to deeper reliance on God's power to deliver us. God's power is like a light shining through human weakness, revealing our basic dependence upon the healing power of Christ's resurrection. Our suffering is ultimately redemptive. However, suffering and persecution could not be endured if it were not for the power of the Holy Spirit, the redemption of Jesus, and the providential care of God.

For This Week:

I want to remember:

I want to put my faith into action by:

Questions to Explore:

Prayer for the Week:

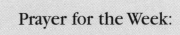

*God, we cry out to you and
we seek your strength and
you look with great kindness
upon your people.
You have lifted us from evil,
showering us with
the graces and blessings
won for us by Jesus.
Hear us now as we look to you
with confidence.
Your mercy is endless and
your love is everlasting!
We praise you,
for you sustain us
throughout each day.
Keep us ever in your caring gaze.
Through Jesus, your Son. Amen.*

Thirteenth Sunday in Ordinary Time

Scripture:

2 Kings 4:8-11, 14-16
Psalm 89:2-3, 16-17, 18-19
Romans 6:3-4, 8-11
Matthew 10:37-42

Focus:

SACRAMENT OF BAPTISM

Reflection:

Directions: *Beside each of the phrases that describe the baptismal encounter with Christ, write a description of what this image means to you from your personal experience as you journey toward initiation or recall your own baptismal living in Christ.*

We . . .

are baptized into Christ

are buried with him

die with Christ

live with him

are alive for God in Christ

Questions:

1. *How has your intimacy with Christ grown and deepened as you walk this journey of faith?*

2. *What ways have you 'died' (your ego, your wants, your control, and your will) with Christ on a daily basis?*

3. *How have you experienced being 'raised up' in Christ by God each day?*

Quotable Quotes:

*Do you not know that all of us who have been baptized
into Christ Jesus were baptized into his death? (Romans 6:3)*

Did You Know?

The word "baptism" in Greek (*baptizein*) means to "plunge" or "immerse" and refers to the ritual action that takes place when the sacrament is celebrated: the one being baptized is immersed into the waters or water is poured over them, completely drenching them. The immersion or drenching takes place three times as the Trinitarian formula is spoken, "I baptize you in the name of the Father, and of the Son, and of the Holy Spirit."

The Church Says:

Baptism is the gateway to the spiritual life, initiating the believer into the community of the faithful and gifting each with a share in the priesthood of all the baptized. Through the sacrament of baptism, we belong to each other in Christ, pouring out our lives in service to one another and offering our baptismal gifts to build up the whole Body of Christ.

Through baptism all sinfulness is wiped away and we are indelibly marked as belonging to Christ. The newly baptized have died with Christ, all past sinfulness cleansed and destroyed, in order to rise with Christ to newness of life. The new life given in baptism endures as an indelible spiritual mark—for our belonging to Christ can never be taken away or revoked, even though we may, in the future, commit mortal sin. (The sacrament of reconciliation is needed by the sinner to address this sin.) Thus, the fruitfulness of baptism may be blocked or hurt by serious sin, but its indelible mark is never destroyed (CCC 1272).

Prior to baptism the individual must give evidence of first faith in Christ. What is being professed and offered in the sacrament of baptism is the faith of the Church—the corporate body. Thus, infants are baptized, because growth and maturity in faith occurs within the loving embrace of the entire household of the faithful. Furthermore, in baptism we are incorporated into Christ's mission, sharing his priestly, prophetic, and kingly role for the sake of the world.

For This Week:

I want to remember:

I want to put my faith into action by:

Questions to Explore:

Prayer for the Week:

*Fill us with
your Spirit that
we may bring Christ to the world.
By your sacrament, we are graced
and gifted to be priest, prophet,
and king
Fill us with your Spirit that
we may bring Christ to the world.
By your sacrament we are
plunged into death's waters.
Fill us with your Spirit that
we may bring Christ to the world.
By your sacrament, we are
bathed, cleansed, and
transformed into new life.
Fill us with your Spirit that
we may bring Christ to the world.
By your sacrament, we are
clothed in Christ.*

*Fill us with
your Spirit that
we may bring Christ to the world.
By your sacrament, we are
enlightened, anointed, and
sealed in your Holy Spirit.
Fill us with your Spirit that
we may bring Christ to the world.
By your sacrament, we are reborn
in Christ.
Fill us with your Spirit that
we may bring Christ to the world.
By your sacrament, we are made
your sons and daughters.
Fill us with your Spirit that
we may bring Christ to the world.
By your sacrament, we are
incorporated into your Body.
Fill us with your Spirit that
we may bring Christ to the world.
Amen.*

Fourteenth Sunday in Ordinary Time

Scripture:

Zechariah 9:9-10
Psalm 145:1-2, 8-9, 10-11, 13-14
Romans 8:9, 11-13
Matthew 11:25-30

Focus:

CHASTITY

Reflection:

Directions: *Think about the image of a yoke, a device that connects two animals together in order that they can work as a team. Reflect on experiences in your life when working as a team was of great benefit. Reflect also on experiences when groups such as committees, cities, countries, worked together as a team to achieve a goal. What do you think Jesus was telling us when he said that his yoke is easy and his burden light?*

Questions:

1. *Describe each of the following:*

    Life according to the Spirit   *Life according to the flesh*

2. *What does it mean for you to live as a chaste person?*

Memorable People:

St. Clare and St. Francis of Assisi were associated in ministry and in religious life and developed a great respect and friendship. They are upheld by the Church as models of chastity.

Aelred of Rievaulx, a Cistercian abbot (c. 1147), wrote extensively, and included in his writings are poems expressing his chaste love for his friend. St. Bernard of Clairvaux wrote regarding the religious life and how the monk might envision himself as the chaste lover serving the Virgin Mary.

Did You Know?

In the Catholic marriage ritual, rings are given as gifts from one spouse to the other and symbolize not only their binding love but also the gift which each one gives to the other of their whole self, as a total togetherness.

Many Catholic Latino wedding celebrations also include additional gifts exchanged as signs of the self-giving and claiming in love of the spouses, such as *arras* (coins, a sign of support for the upkeep of the household), the *lazo* (lasso, a sign of undivided love), the Bible (a sign of the strength they will derive from the Word of God), and a rosary (a sign of their need for prayer).

The Church Says:

The Spirit of God, a God who is love, dwelling in each of us, has inscribed upon the human heart not only the capacity to love and share and reach out in communion but the vocation or calling to do so. There is integrity to the way in which God creates people, a connection between what we feel, who we are, and how we are built, that leads us to this vocation. All that we are is subordinated to the ultimate end of humanity and creation itself, that is, to live in Christ.

The Church upholds virtuous love or chastity for all human beings. The human person learns to govern passions, desires, and drives—living according to the Spirit—or that person is dominated and overwhelmed by them and acts without true direction ordered toward the kingdom—living according to the flesh. The Church's understanding of the virtue of chastity must be seen in the context of one's sexual identity, for God created male and female, each with an equal dignity.

For This Week:

I want to remember:

I want to put my faith into action by:

Questions to Explore:

Prayer for the Week:

Spirit of God,
permeate us with your love
that we might come to understand
the expansive, unconditional love of God
for all living beings.
Led by your love,
create in us a deep respect
and care for others.
Integrate us and make us whole,
a holy vessel of love,
that we might reach out
to brother and sister alike,
in mutual sharing of body, mind,
spirit, and soul.
Amen.

Fifteenth Sunday in Ordinary Time

Scripture:

Isaiah 55:10-11
Psalm 65:10, 11, 12-13, 14
Romans 8:18-23
Matthew 13:1-23

Focus:

SACRED SCRIPTURE

Reflection:

Directions: *Select one of the scripture phrases below that appeals to your spirit. Then indicate the ripple effect of this Word in your life. Begin by choosing a verse and writing it in the center of the circles. Allow it to roll through your imagination and soul for a short time. Around the first circle write whatever comes to mind. Then think about what you have written and allow these ideas to flow through your spirit. When a new insight comes to mind, write these thoughts and feelings in the second circle. Continue in this manner until you feel you have written down all your thoughts, feelings, or insights. Then look back at what you wrote and allow the fruit of the Word to bring you to new depths of wisdom.*

"To you has been given a knowledge of the mysteries of the reign of God."

"You have visited the land and watered it; greatly have you enriched it."

"Blest are your eyes because they see and blest are your ears because they hear."

"My word shall not return to me void."

"The whole created world eagerly awaits the revelation of the sons of God."

"The seed that falls on good ground will yield a fruitful harvest."

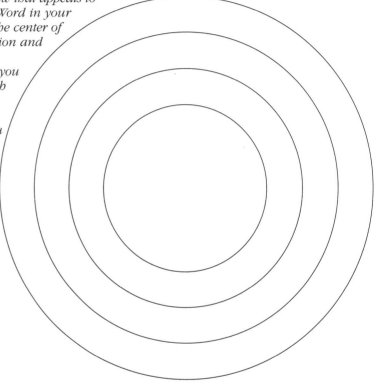

Questions:

1. *Why read the scriptures?*

2. *How has the Word of God come alive for you as you experience these sessions?*

Did You Know?

Three significant realities are "given" in a symbolic fashion to catechumens when they enter the catechumenate stage of the initiation process: They are signed with the cross; the community of the faithful welcomes them; and they are handed the Word of God. The Lectionary, the book of lessons from sacred scripture arranged for proclamation at Mass and other occasions, is the basis and heart of their instruction and reflection throughout the period of the catechumenate.

The Church Says:

The Church teaches that to faithfully interpret scripture one must read it holistically and from within the tradition. What does this mean? First, in the interpretation of scripture one must be very attentive to its whole content and unity of purpose. The individual books of the Bible are different, yet there is a unity and wholeness to all of them together. They revolve around the center and heart of God's plan for us who is Jesus Christ. Second, scripture must be read and understood within the living tradition of the community of the faithful. The Second Vatican Council taught that both scripture and tradition flow out of the same font, divine revelation. Both are in dialogue with each other. Together scripture and tradition make up one single "deposit of the Word of God, which is entrusted to the Church" (DV 10). Thus, we believe that the authentic interpretation of the Word of God, whether in its written form or in the tradition, has been given to the living teaching office of the Church. This teaching authority comes from Jesus and therefore is not superior to the Word but is its servant.

Catholics hold that sacred scripture is food for our souls, a font from which we might draw strength for nourishing our faith. Therefore, the Second Vatican Council urged that all members of the Church should have as wide an access as possible to sacred scripture. The ministry of the Word is carried out in the Catholic Church through homilies, pastoral preaching, catechesis, and every other form of instruction, including this process of initiation. Every member of the Church is called to a frequent reading and study of sacred scripture for, echoing St. Jerome, the Second Vatican Council taught, "Ignorance of the scriptures is ignorance of Christ" (DV 25; cf. St. Jerome, Comm. in Isaiah, Prol.: PL 24, 17).

For This Week:

I want to remember:

I want to put my faith into action by:

Questions to Explore:

Prayer for the Week:

God, living Word,
who came to dwell among your people,
open us to hear your Word.
May our encounter with you in the Word
be food for our souls.
Plant your Word deep in our beings
that we might be encouraged,
instructed, and formed
into a people of the Word.
You have revealed yourself to us
in the Word.
Let us deepen our knowing
that the Word might become
a seed planted in fertile soil,
yielding a rich and
abundant harvest in us—
food for a hungry world. Amen.

Sixteenth Sunday in Ordinary Time

Scripture:

Wisdom 12:13, 16-19
Psalm 86:5-6, 9-10, 15-16
Romans 8:26-27
Matthew 13:24-43
    [or 13:24-30 (short form)]

Focus:

THE PROBLEM OF MORAL EVIL

Reflection:

Directions: *Rewrite one of the parables from today's gospel (the weeds among the wheat, the mustard seed, or the yeast in the bread dough) in the light of your own experience and understanding of the Church's teaching on moral evil.*

Questions:

Describe an experience that is or was a real struggle between good and evil for you.

1. *What made it a struggle? What made evil so desirable and good so difficult to choose?*

2. *What did you freely choose to do? Why? What has happened as a result of your choice?*

Memorable People:

The Cathedral of Santiago de Compostela (Spain) is an extremely important pilgrimage site—legend has it that the remains of St. James were found in Jerusalem and transferred eventually to this cathedral. The original edifice was destroyed by the Moors in 997 but was rebuilt and consecrated in 1211. It is a magnificent church that incorporates various styles, both Baroque and Romanesque, in a cross-shaped structure. An ornate silver censor hangs upon an immense chain from its ceiling. On the feast of St. James and on other special occasions, the censor is filled with incense and eight or ten men pull the guide ropes which then begin to swing the censor back and forth above the heads of the assembly as it flies from one transept to the other (that is, from one arm of the cross to the other). The use of incense in our Catholic tradition has been to give honor to sacred objects. In this case, as whenever the worshiping assembly is incensed, honor is being accorded to the holy gathering of the faithful. The very way in which this massive medieval censor is used in this cruciform pilgrimage cathedral seems to symbolize that, by the sacrifice of Jesus, the possibility of holiness is held out to us. In the very gathering of the faithful, under the sign of God's love, all forms of evil are banished.

Did You Know?

The Old Testament records many instances where the image "lamb" is referred to as a sacrifice, oblation, or an offering for sin. The New Testament authors build on this image and apply it to Christ, who died for our sins. Christian iconography from the earliest times, therefore, depicted Jesus Christ as the "Lamb of God," frequently holding the banner of victory—denoting the resurrection.

The Church Says:

There is a type of evil that we choose to engage in, either by action or inaction. At the end of the world all will be judged accordingly. The idea of moral evil rests upon the foundation of free choice. The Church believes that human beings are accountable and therefore move toward final destiny by their choice, through the exercise of free will. A quick recounting of history is ample proof that human beings have chosen to do wrong, and thus sinned against God and neighbor. Indeed, moral evil creates havoc more harmful to our well-being than even the suffering caused by physical evil such as earthquakes, hurricanes, and tornadoes.

From early on in our Christian history, our greatest theologians have asserted that God is neither directly nor indirectly responsible for the cause of moral evil in the world. Saint Augustine and Saint Thomas upheld that God, by the divine nature, directs the human heart toward good. The responsibility for choosing other than the good does not belong to God, but to human beings. The Second Vatican Council declared that in our very depths human beings are divided, frequently gravitating toward what is wrong and sinking into evil ways. God is neither directly nor indirectly the author or cause of evil; in addition, God is always "on our side," championing the good in us, and working for our well-being. The provident goodness of God works for good in everything, including those events and actions when we choose to do wrong.

The discussion of why evil exists is not easily answered but can only be resolved by the totality of faith. The goodness of creation, the patient, merciful love of the Most High, the beauty of God's covenant with us, the Word made flesh, Jesus who saves us, the transforming fire of the Holy Spirit, the birth of the Church, the continual gathering of the faithful, and the nourishment of life-giving sacraments all attest to our end and goal in the goodness of the divine One who provides for us and who seeks us out no matter how far we have fallen.

For This Week:

I want to remember:

I want to put my faith into action by:

Questions to Explore:

Prayer for the Week:

Merciful God,
my life is littered with the weeds
of the evil I choose
in spite of the abundant goodness
of your grace.
Illuminate my heart
and purify my will
that I might be empowered
by your great love and leniency
to choose your will over my own.
When evil befalls me,
strengthen me
that I might watch and wait
for the goodness
hidden among the thorns of pain.
Grant me this prayer in the name of Jesus.
Amen.

Seventeenth Sunday in Ordinary Time

Scripture:

1 Kings 3:5, 7-12
Psalm 119:57, 72, 76-77, 127-128, 129-130
Romans 8:28-30
Matthew 13:44-52

Focus:

THE KINGDOM OF GOD

Reflection:

Directions: *Today's gospel presents three images of God's reign: The Buried Treasure, The Valuable Pearl, and The Dragnet. In the first two, the people who discovered them gave all that they had to buy the field with the treasure and the valuable pearl. Write in the space below your responses to the following questions:*

Questions:

1. *Have you ever given yourself completely to something or someone?*

2. *Can you imagine giving yourself completely over to God?*

3. *What holds you back?*

Memorable People:

St. Ignatius Loyola, 1491-1556, founder of the Jesuits, in his *Spiritual Exercises* presents meditations on what it means to choose to live in Jesus' kingdom versus the kingdom of evil (that of the devil). Ignatius himself was drawn to live the fullness of the Christian life through growth in humility and poverty, desiring God's grace above any human attachment of the ego. His feast day is celebrated July 31.

Did You Know?

The Greek word *basileia* (meaning "kingdom") is the root of *basilica*, a building for certain public, official uses in ancient Rome. This basilica style of public building was eventually adapted for use by the early Church for its larger and more lavish worship spaces. A basilica church holds a special significance for a particular people or area. Today the major basilicas are located in Rome. Other church buildings throughout the world are given "minor" basilica status by the Vatican.

The Church Says:

The phrase "kingdom of God," also translated as "reign of God," "dominion of God," and "kingdom of heaven," occurs 150 times in the New Testament. The expression has roots in the Old Testament as well. Jesus announces the reign of God, and through his ministry and mission invites all people to enter into it. In spreading God's kingdom, Jesus extended his saving mission to all without limit. Included are the poor and lowly, the outcasts of society, the sick, and the sinful. Jesus offers an experience of salvation for all.

God's kingdom is here and now, yet is not fully realized. Jesus is the fulfillment for all time of God's love lavished upon the world. Jesus' transfiguration is a foretaste of when all drawn to Christ will be transformed in glory. Those transformed in glory must first bear hardship and possibly persecution and the cross.

Jesus, who had a vivid sense of God's presence, invites us into this same union with God. Being united with God involves extending compassion to the weak, insignificant, the lost, and the lowly. Thus, union with God requires personal appropriation through concrete decisions and actions in a radical ongoing conversion.

The Church, though not synonymous with the kingdom of God, is founded on God's reign with Christ as its head. The Church is to participate in Christ's mission to bring about the reign of God in this world.

For This Week:

I want to remember:

I want to put my faith into action by:

Questions to Explore:

Prayer for the Week:

Good and gracious God,
give me a heart that is wise
and understanding
like Solomon's heart.
Take from me
my false perception of what is good.
Remove the barriers
of materialism, pride, and fear
that prevent me from selling all
to receive the treasure you offer.
Give me compassion to love and accept
all of my sisters and brothers
whom you invite to your kingdom
with me.
Place in my heart a desire for you alone.
Amen.

Eighteenth Sunday in Ordinary Time

Scripture:

Isaiah 55:1-3
Psalm 145:8-9, 15-16, 17-18
Romans 8:35, 37-39
Matthew 14:13-21

Focus:

EUCHARIST AS MEAL

Reflection:

Directions: Spend some time letting the hungers of your heart come to consciousness. Complete the following phrase with as many responses as arise within you:

> *I hunger for . . .*

Questions:

1. *How has God satisfied your needs? When have you experienced abundant generosity from God in satisfying your hungers?*

2. *As a disciple of Jesus, describe some of the ways you are asked by God to feed others.*

Memorable People:

St. Tarsicius, a young altar boy who lived in the fourth century, took the Eucharist to Christians in prison. He risked his life during this time of persecution so that they could share in the eucharistic meal. He eventually was stoned to death on one such mission. He is the patron saint of first communicants. His feast day is August 15.

Did You Know?

The earliest depiction of the miraculous feeding of the multitude is found on the "Trinity" sarcophagus (c. 315), a stone coffin, now found in the Lateran museum in Rome. The name "Trinity" is used since three images are presented: the miracle of Cana on the left, the miraculous feeding in the center, and the raising of Lazarus on the right.

The original intention of reserving the Eucharist was so that communion could be taken to the sick who were not able to participate in the Eucharist with the Sunday assembly. The Church began this practice out of the belief that weekly partaking of the eucharistic meal is necessary nourishment for all believers.

The Church Says:

The Eucharist is the third and final sacrament of initiation. The Eucharist, the Lord's Supper, is at once a memorial, a sacrifice, thanksgiving, an impetus for mission, and a meal. The Second Vatican Council renewed the focus on Eucharist as a meal. The Church instructs that bread that looks like bread be used for the Eucharist, and prefers the faithful to partake of both bread and wine as a fuller experience of sharing the meal of the Lord's Supper.

Eucharist is an intimate communion with Christ and, thus, a sharing of the sacrifice and death of Christ. Eucharist is necessary to nourish the spiritual life of all believers. The Church encourages the faithful to receive Eucharist every Sunday. The Eucharist is always celebrated and partaken of in the midst of the gathered assembly, who signify the presence of Christ. At Mass the community gathers, hears and reflects on the Word of God, offers intercession for God's people, presents bread and wine, and shares in the action of Christ who "took, blessed, broke, and gave" bread (Matthew 14:18).

The Eucharist draws us to the eternal heavenly banquet, the supper of the Lamb, the wedding banquet with Christ the bridegroom. Sharing in the eucharistic meal makes us one body in Christ. Those who share in this meal are then sent forth to feed others as they have been fed.

For This Week:

I want to remember:

I want to put my faith into action by:

Questions to Explore:

Prayer for the Week:

Gracious God, you provide
*   a rich feast for us.*
You bid us come to your abundant table.
You feed our hearts as no other can.
When we are slow to respond to your invitation,
*   make our hunger for you grow.*
Give us a hunger for nothing less than you.
As you feed us,
*   give us hearts that see*
*   the hunger in our sisters and brothers.*
Never let us be satisfied
*   until the rich and poor,*
*   the happy and sad,*
*   the prominent and forgotten,*
*   share together the food you offer.*
Amen.

Nineteenth Sunday in Ordinary Time

Scripture:

1 Kings 19:9, 11-13
Psalm 85:9, 10, 11-12, 13-14
Romans 9:1-5
Matthew 14:22-33

Focus:

REVELATION

Reflection:

Directions: The key moments, listed below, indicate the progression of the stories presented in the first reading and the gospel. As you look through them, select the passage—Elijah or the Storm at Sea—that seems to reflect your life right now. Then write down the parallels between your life and the key moments from the scripture story.

ELIJAH

Fled to Mt. Horeb

Hid in a cave

Listened for God in the windstorm

Sought God in the earthquake

Expected to hear God in the fire

To his surprise, found God in a tiny whispering sound

Hid his face in a cloak, standing at the entrance of the cave

THE STORM AT SEA

Jesus left them to pray

The boat is tossed about by a storm

Jesus came walking to them on the water

They feared it was a ghost

Peter recognized the Lord

Peter walks to Jesus on the water

He became frightened and began to sink

Jesus stretched out his hand to save him

How little faith you have

The wind died down after Jesus climbed into the boat

You are the Son of God!

Quotable Quotes:

In speaking of the certainty of faith, in spite of revelation being mysterious, John Henry Cardinal Newman (1801-1890) wrote, "Ten thousand difficulties do not make one doubt."
(*Apologia pro Vita Sua*, London, Longman, 1878, p. 239)

Memorable People:

The great medieval mystic St. John of the Cross (d. 1591) wrote, "Any person questioning God or desiring some vision or revelation would be guilty not only of foolish behavior but also of offending him, by not fixing his eyes entirely upon Christ and by living with the desire of some other novelty." (*The Ascent of Mount Carmel*, 2, 22, 3-5, in *The Collected Works*, trsl. K. Kavanaugh, OCD, and O. Rodriguez, OCD, Washington, D.C., Institute of Carmelite Studies, 1979)

The Church Says:

The bishops of the world at the Second Vatican Council wrote, "It pleased God, in his goodness and wisdom, to reveal himself and to make known the mystery of his will (cf. Ephesians 1:9). His will was that [humanity] should have access to the Father, through Christ, the Word made flesh, in the Holy Spirit, and thus become sharers in the divine nature. . . . By this revelation, then, the invisible God . . . from the fullness of his love, addresses [us] as his friends and moves among [us] . . . in order to invite and receive [us] into his own company" (DV 2). This self-disclosure of God is summed up in Christ, who is proclaimed by the Church as both the mediator and fulfillment of divine revelation. Thus, while the Church holds that God is revealed in creation (CCC 54), and in the history of the chosen people from the time of Abraham (CCC 60), and throughout the history of Israel and the first covenant (CCC 61-4), the fullness of God's Word to us is communicated in Jesus Christ (CCC 65). Thus, everything God speaks to us is spoken in Christ.

To understand, as Catholics do, that the fullness of revelation is encompassed by Jesus who is "the way, the truth, and the life" (John 14:6) does not mean that the self-disclosure of God to us is not sometimes obscure or mysterious (CCC 157). What has been revealed and how that forms our faith is certain, but human language and thought may struggle to express and articulate what is known of the divine in the relationship of love communicated by God's self-disclosure. The result is that we live now within the promise of God. Human life has as its goal the ultimate union with God who has loved us so much that the divine reaches out to us and communicates. A relationship is established that puts before us a future filled with justice, hope, love, and the vindication of faith. The eternal Word, Jesus Christ, who opens this avenue of promise, is experienced in the proclamation and study of sacred scripture, in the body of believers, the Church, and in the living tradition that is handed on by the Church from age to age.

For This Week:

I want to remember:

I want to put my faith into action by:

Questions to Explore:

Prayer for the Week:

God, you come to me
in the stillness of the whispering wind in the trees;
you are with me at this moment and as I walk
through each day.
When my heart is afraid you are there to quiet
my fears and reassure me of your abiding
presence. In the chaos and storms of my life you
have reached out your hand to me and steadied
my faltering steps.
God, how can I express my gratitude at your
desire to make yourself known to me? How can I
deepen my faith as I let go of my worries and
weaknesses?
Teach me, Lord, and excite my soul to discover
more of your revelation to me through a fervor for
your sacred scriptures and a commitment to the
silence of prayer. Empower me with the ardor of
your Holy Spirit. Amen.

Twentieth Sunday in Ordinary Time

Scripture:

Isaiah 56:1, 6-7
Psalm 67:2-3, 5, 6, 8
Romans 11:13-15, 29-32
Matthew 15:21-28

Focus:

SACRAMENT OF ANOINTING OF THE SICK

Reflection:

Directions: *In the reflection on your experiences of exclusion in your childhood, write about such an incident. Describe your feelings or thoughts of being excluded. Then describe your thoughts or feelings, as you recall the times you were included.*

Questions:

1. *If you had been an Israelite in the setting of the first reading from Isaiah, how might you have responded to the prophet's words that these foreigners are also called to be God's chosen people?*

2. *How would you react to the proclamation that their holocausts and sacrifices are also acceptable on God's altar?*

3. *Describe a similar incident in today's world.*

Quotable Quotes:

In the document on the Church, the bishops of the world at the Second Vatican Council said, "By the sacred anointing of the sick and the prayer of the priests, the whole Church commends those who are ill to the suffering and glorified Lord that he may raise them up and save them. And indeed she exhorts them to contribute to the good of the People of God by freely uniting themselves to the passion and death of Christ."

Did You Know?

Viaticum, one particular ritual practice for those who are sick, is the final Holy Communion which is provided for them. "Viaticum" means "food for the journey" and thus indicates our belief that life does not end in death and that those believers who suffer and die receive new life and victory in the Lord Jesus.

The Church Says:

The Catholic Church does not believe that sickness is a punishment from God, for the Son of God has made our pain his own. The Lamb of God, sacrificed for us, takes away the sin of the world. Thus, by the mystery of his own suffering and death, Jesus gives new meaning to our own illness and suffering whose earthly reality is transformed by the Lord. Those who are sick—and indeed all those who are healthy—can look upon the cross of Christ and know that humanity in its limitations and sickness has been configured and united to the Lord of life who is the redeemer.

In the sacrament of anointing of the sick the Church supports by prayer and presence persons who are sick and invites them to faith in Jesus—in spite of the burdens and doubts occasioned by sickness. The Church understands and upholds that through the celebration of this sacrament persons who are sick are strengthened through the grace of God and given peace and courage, even if they are not totally physically healed of their debilitating condition. As Catholics, we believe that suffering and sickness, through the witness of the Church to the gospel, can acquire a transforming power.

It is for this reason that this sacrament should always be proceeded by the Word of God (except in emergency) and be celebrated communally, with the sick person surrounded by family, friends, and other believers. Even if the sacrament is celebrated by a priest alone with the person who is sick, the communion of saints, the whole household of the faith, is present in prayer, consoling, reaching out, and touching with this ritual action.

For This Week:

I want to remember:

I want to put my faith into action by:

Questions to Explore:

Prayer for the Week:

Father, your Son accepted our sufferings
*   to teach us the virtue of patience in human illness.*
Hear the prayers we offer for our sick brother/sister . . .
*   (name those who are ill)*
May all who suffer pain, illness, or disease
*   realize that they have been chosen*
*   to be saints and know that*
*   they are joined to Christ*
*   in his suffering for the salvation of the world.*
We ask this through Christ our Lord.
Amen.

(Prayer from Pastoral Care of the Sick)

Twenty-first Sunday in Ordinary Time

Scripture:

Isaiah 22:15, 19-23
Psalm 138:1-2, 2-3, 6, 8
Romans 11:33-36
Matthew 16:13-20

Focus:

PETRINE MINISTRY IN THE CHURCH

Reflection:

Directions: *In the space provided, list several situations in your life where you exercise authority (family, work, community, or Church). After each situation, enumerate the responsibilities that accompany this authority. At the end of your list, describe how you carry out your role of authority, which flows from God, in a manner that befits this sacred trust.*

Questions:

1. *How does the ministry of the pope affect you from the perspective of his influence as a world leader?*

2. *What changes regarding the influence of Petrine ministry on your life do you anticipate as you prepare to accept papal leadership as a member of the Catholic community?*

3. *The source of human authority is God. What does it mean when we define Church authority as shepherding, stewardship and ministry?*

Memorable People:

Pope John XXIII called the bishops of the world together, convening the Second Vatican Council as a "new Pentecost" to open wide the windows and doors of the Church to the activity of the Holy Spirit. Suffering from stomach cancer, he died in 1962 while the council was still in session. Pope Paul VI continued the enormous self-renewing agenda of the council and guided the Church through her difficult post-Vatican II transition. His great papal encyclical, *On Evangelization in the Modern World,* exhorted the laity to take up their baptismal call and proclaim the Good News to the entire world.

Did You Know?

The word "pope" comes from the Latin *papa,* an affectionate term for "father." From about the sixth century, the term *papa* was applied to the bishop of Rome. Other papal titles indicate the unique position the bishop of Rome has in the Church: Vicar of Jesus Christ, Successor of the Chief of the Apostles, Supreme Pontiff of the Universal Church, Patriarch of the West, Primate of Italy, Archbishop and Metropolitan of the Roman Province, Sovereign of the State of Vatican City, and Servant of the Servants of God.

The Church Says:

Peter is understood by the Church as first among equals, a foundational leader. This image echoes today's gospel passage where Jesus describes Peter as "rock" (Matthew 16:18). Peter confesses his faith in Jesus as the Christ, the Son of God, and the anointed Messiah. Paul takes up this same theme immediately after his conversion as he begins his own evangelizing ministry.

Although the bishop who sits in the chair of Peter presides over the entire Church in charity, responsibility for shepherding does not rest with the bishop of Rome alone. Jesus called to himself the Twelve, and this apostolic witness and function in the Church is given to all the bishops of the world who together with their head, the pope, exercise their shepherding office collegially. The Second Vatican Council, however, upheld the primacy of the pope, declaring in the document, *Lumen gentium* (The Light of the World): "For the Roman Pontiff, by reason of his office as Vicar of Christ, namely, and as pastor of the entire Church, has full, supreme and universal power over the whole Church, a power which he can always exercise unhindered. The order of bishops is the successor to the college of the apostles in their role as teachers and pastors, and in it the apostolic college is perpetuated. Together with their head, the Supreme Pontiff, and never apart from him, they have supreme and full authority over the universal Church; but this power cannot be exercised without the agreement of the Roman Pontiff" (LG 22).

For This Week:

I want to remember:

I want to put my faith into action by:

Questions to Explore:	Prayer for the Week:
	God of wisdom,
	* who can understand*
	* or pretend to know your ways?*
	Your knowledge is beyond
	* our human capacity to understand.*
	Yet throughout the ages
	* you have guided us and proved to be*
	* faithful and trustworthy.*
	Be with us and strengthen our faith in you.
	Reveal to us our responsibilities
	* as stewards of this beautiful earth*
	* and all that you created in the universe.*
	Give us the courage to place our trust
	* totally in your divine ways.*
	We confess to you and to one another
	* that from you and through you*
	* all things are.*
	All glory and praise be yours.
	Amen.

Twenty-second Sunday in Ordinary Time

Scripture:

Jeremiah 20:7-9
Psalm 63:2, 3-4, 5-6, 8-9
Romans 12:1-2
Matthew 16:21-27

Focus:

THE CROSS IN THE LIFE OF THE DISCIPLE

Reflection:

Directions: *Jesus says that to follow him you must deny yourself and take up the cross in your own life. Recall the crosses you have carried in your own life. Some may be small, and others large. In carrying a cross, a part of one's self is denied. Reflect on what part of you was denied in carrying each cross. Write as many as come to mind in the space below.*

Crosses I Have Carried   The Part of Myself I Denied

Jesus also says that in losing your life for his sake, you will find life. Give examples of the life you have gained through carrying the cross.

The Life I Have Gained

Questions:

1. *In your experience of taking up your cross, what feelings emerged?*

2. *What new insights about the meaning of the cross did you discover in this reflection?*

3. *What cross do you face at this time in your life?*

Quotable Quotes:

St. Paul of the Cross (1694-1775) in 1720 founded the religious order known as the Passionists, who, in addition to the traditional vows of poverty, chastity, and obedience, take a fourth vow to promote devotion to the passion of Jesus. He wrote, "In naked faith and without images, clothe yourself always in the sufferings of Jesus. It is love which unites and which makes our own the sufferings of the one we love. It is through love that you will make the sufferings of Jesus your own." (*In the heart of God: The Spiritual Teaching of Saint Paul of the Cross,* found in *The Heart of Catholicism,* Theodore E. James, ed., Our Sunday Visitor, Inc., Huntington, Indiana, 1997, p. 493)

Did You Know?

The Way of the Cross or the Stations of the Cross is a Catholic devotion that originated in the pilgrimage to Jerusalem to retrace the steps of Jesus during his passion. This devotion, originating in the fifteenth century and encouraged by Franciscans, consists of fourteen stations with a cross at each station. An artistic rendition of various aspects of the passion usually accompanies each station. Specific prayers are recited before each station as the participants meditate on that aspect of the passion of Jesus.

The Church Says:

Christians follow Jesus, who found true life by living a life faithful to God, even when this faithfulness led to humiliation, torture, and death in the cruel Roman method of crucifixion. As Jesus' faithfulness brought him through death to the resurrection, disciples in faith see the cross as a path to resurrection and new life.

John Paul II, who himself shared in the suffering of Christ through an assassination attempt, stated that through the passion of Christ all human suffering has the potential to be transformed. Suffering in itself is not redemptive. But consciously uniting one's own suffering with Christ's passion and death allows one to share in the new life of Christ's resurrection. The paschal mystery, Christ's passion, death, and resurrection, becomes the way of life for all Christians.

John Paul II created the term "the gospel of suffering." In dying on the cross, Christ reached the very roots of evil, of sin and death, and makes it possible to transform suffering into good through the saving power of love. Through the heart of the experience of suffering and the cross, we are led into God's kingdom. Taking up one's cross is a matter of the heart, the inner spirit, and love.

As part of the Good Friday liturgy, Catholics venerate the "wood" of the cross, rather than the crucifix, through a kiss, genuflection, bow, or simple touch showing our willingness to embrace the cross in our lives as Jesus did.

For This Week:

I want to remember:

I want to put my faith into action by:

Questions to Explore:

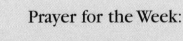

Prayer for the Week:

Loving and gracious God,
you dupe me with your love.
The life you offer is more than I can resist.
Continue to call me to you.
Teach my heart the way of your heart.
Give me the willingness to embrace
the crosses that come into my life.
Unite me ever more fully with Christ,
whose faithful living
shows me the way to fuller life.
I pray in union with Christ,
who died and is risen.
Amen.

Twenty-third Sunday in Ordinary Time

Scripture:

Ezekiel 33:7-9
Psalm 95:1-2, 6-7, 8-9
Romans 13:8-10
Matthew 18:15-20

Focus:

CONVERSION

Reflection:

Directions: *Conversion means a change of heart, literally a turning or change in direction of one's life. Look back over your life and recall a particular time when you experienced God leading you to and through this change. Respond to the following as a way of reflecting on your conversion experience:*

I changed from . . .

to . . .

Before the conversion, I was . . .

I felt . . .

For awhile, I resisted this conversion or change because . . .

After the conversion, I was . . .

I felt . . .

God invited me to this conversion by . . .

Quotable Quotes:

St. Francis de Sales (1567-1622), bishop of Geneva, wrote a spirituality of the laity in his *Introduction to the Devout Life* (1609). He writes, "True and living devotion . . . presupposes the love of God. . . . Devotion must be practiced differently by the gentleman, the artisan, the valet, the prince, the widow, the daughter, the married woman. [Indeed,] the practice of devotion must be accommodated to the strength, the concerns and the duties of each individual" (*Introduction to the Devout Life*, found in *How to Read Church History*, vol. 2, Jean Comby with Diarmaid MacCulloch, Crossroad, New York, 1986, M. Lydamore and J. Bowden, trsl., p. 36).

Memorable People:

St. Augustine's autobiography, *The Confessions,* includes the story of his conversion, which took place after much searching, many struggles, and with the constant support of his mother, St. Monica, who for years prayed for his conversion. After his conversion from his dissolute lifestyle, St. Augustine (d. 430) went on to become bishop of Hippo in North Africa and one of the greatest theologians and teachers that the Church has ever known. St. Monica's feast is August 27, followed by the feast of St. Augustine on August 28.

St. Paul, formerly known as Saul of Tarsus who persecuted Christians, became an apostle after his powerful conversion told in Acts of the Apostles 9:1-19.

The Church Says:

God calls all followers of Christ to a life of conversion. Conversion literally means a change in direction of how one lives. Conversion includes both an interior change of heart, thought, and will (*metanoia*), and an exterior change in action (*epistrophe*).

St. Paul and St. Augustine (d. 430) both had significant conversions, which point to a fourfold pattern of conversion: (1) a tension in one's life, (2) a learning or insight from one's past life, (3) an experience of mercy or forgiveness, and (4) the gracious call from God to a new way of life. The experience of conversion is initiated by God's gracious action.

Conversion in Christ is always communal. Though a personal experience, the individual's faith is affected by and affects the faith of others. The Church together is called to walk the ongoing path of conversion, of purification and enlightenment. Living one's faith necessarily includes being involved in the conversion process of others.

The seven sacraments help the believer become transformed in love. After faltering, through the sacrament of reconciliation the believer is able to begin the journey anew and take heart in God's saving love.

The aim of Christian conversion is for the believer's whole being to be converted to Christ, and manifested through visible signs, gestures, and works. For a Christian, the ongoing relationship with Christ is central and continually invites the believer not only to keep the commandments, but to embrace love even when this entails self-denial.

For This Week:

I want to remember:

I want to put my faith into action by:

Questions to Explore:

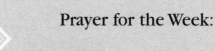

Prayer for the Week:

God, ever faithful,
open my inner spirit to you more deeply.
God, ever loving,
help me to let go of my hurts,
guilt, and resentments.
God, ever merciful,
heal and free me
from all that keeps me chained and bound.
God, ever gracious,
give me and all of my sisters and brothers
what we need to live more fully
as your people of faith.
I pray through, with, and in Jesus.
Amen.

Twenty-fourth Sunday in Ordinary Time

Scripture:

Sirach 27:30–28:7
Psalm 103:1-2, 3-4, 9-10, 11-12
Romans 14:7-9
Matthew 18:21-35

Focus:

FORGIVENESS

Reflection:

Directions: Reflect upon the four fundamental teachings that inspire believers to forgive, listed below. Then think of a person who has treated you unjustly and caused you suffering and pain. Under each of the beliefs write down how this inspires you to begin the process of forgiving this person.

God's mercy is without limit. God's love is given without our merit.

How can we say that we love God and hate another, when all people are one in the Lord—when God made everyone in God's image and likeness?

We dare to pray, "Forgive us our trespasses as we forgive those who trespass against us."

Jesus suffered and died, forgiving even those who crucified him.

Questions:

1. *What happened in your heart as you worked through this process of forgiveness?*

2. *How does lack of forgiveness hold you captive?*

3. *What does this teaching on forgiveness imply for the world community?*

Quotable Quotes:

Forgive your neighbor the wrong he has done, and then your sins will be pardoned when you pray. (Sirach 28:2)

Did You Know?

In their proximate period of preparation for full initiation, called the period of Purification and Enlightenment, adults are presented with the Lord's Prayer. This presentation, for pastoral reasons, may be made during the preceding period, the Catechumenate. This prayer text, the Church believes, is proper to those who have been baptized and expresses their new spirit of adoption by God (RCIA 149). It will be prayed by the newly baptized for the first time in the eucharistic assembly, which is a gathering of those who have been redeemed and forgiven and who therefore extend this mercy of God to others.

The Church Says:

The ability to forgive begins with our understanding and belief in the limitless mercy and love of God. Furthermore, the Church teaches that the baptized, having experienced this mercy and forgiveness through the redemption of Jesus, are expected and commanded to forgive one another.

Recall that in Jesus' teaching on prayer, he instructed his followers and us to pray, "Forgive us our trespasses as we forgive those who trespass against us." This is a difficult command, but it is clear that Jesus challenges us to "love, even our enemies, and pray for those who persecute us, that we may be children of our heavenly Father" (Matthew 5:44 adapted). Forgiveness that is without limits or reservations can only begin in prayer. As we pray to become molded in the image of Christ the path of reconciliation opens us to love, conquering even the worst injustice.

Equally powerful in illuminating our hearts to forgive our enemies is meditation upon the passion and sacrifice of Jesus who could say from the cross, "Father, forgive them, for they know not what they do." Thus, the unmerited and unlimited mercy of God, the desire on the part of the believer to be forgiven by God, prayer, and the passion of Jesus enliven our spirits to begin the process of forgiveness.

For This Week:

I want to remember:

I want to put my faith into action by:

Questions to Explore:

Prayer for the Week:

God of Mercy,
in your wisdom you encourage us
to forgive our neighbor's injustice.
We hold on tight to our anger
and vengeful thoughts
but your love compels us to let these go.
We nourish anger against our enemies
and yet we seek your healing.
We refuse to extend mercy to those
who have hurt us,
yet we seek your pardon.
Open our tight fists of wrath
and teach us to set enmity aside,
remembering that we are
joined with our sisters and brothers in Christ.
Strengthen us in the power of Jesus' death
and resurrection, we pray.
Amen.

Twenty-fifth Sunday in Ordinary Time

Scripture:

Isaiah 55:6-9
Psalm 145:2-3, 8-9, 17-18
Philippians 1:20-24, 27
Matthew 20:1-16

Focus:

THE SACRAMENT OF PENANCE

Reflection:

Directions: *Spend some time reflecting on the past week:*

Ask the Holy Spirit to guide you.

Think of the blessings, people, or events of the week. Thank God for these.

Think of actions done or not done, words spoken or unspoken, which were sinful, and ask God for forgiveness, healing, and strength to overcome them.

Think of actions done to you or words said against you by others and forgive those who sinned against you and pray for them.

Speak to God in the quiet of your heart or pray a favorite prayer or psalm.

Questions:

In the gospel, Matthew 20:1-16:

1. *How would you have felt if you had been one of the first chosen?*

2. *How would you have felt if you had been one of the last chosen?*

3. *How would you describe the employer's hiring and wage practices?*

Did You Know?

There are four parts to the celebration of the sacrament of reconciliation:

1. The believer, with sorrow and contrition for having sinned, expresses the love of God which has moved one to celebrate the sacrament. In addition, we must have a firm resolution to avoid sin in the future.

2. The sins themselves are admitted. This is always done privately to a priest who presides over the celebration of this sacrament. This private and secret nature of confession is called "the sacramental seal"; thus, the priest cannot make use of or reveal under any circumstances what has been admitted by the individual.

3. The wrong that is done in sinning must be compensated and therefore satisfaction offered. This is also known as penance. While frequently this penance is observed by praying, it can also extend to concrete activities of charitable works, service to one's neighbor, and/or voluntary self-sacrifice.

4. The priest extends his hands over the head of the believer in blessing and prays the absolution prayer, which expresses that God alone forgives and reconciles the sinner to himself and to the Church.

The Church Says:

God loves us completely and unconditionally and from that abundance flows the forgiveness of sins. It is in Jesus Christ that this divine love is fully manifested. The life, ministry, suffering, death, and resurrection of Jesus unlocks for us the font of new, risen, healed life as we are incorporated into the mystery of Christ and his Church in baptism. Baptism takes away all sin. Those who fall into sin after baptism are not baptized again, but instead experience the bountiful mercy and forgiveness of God in the sacrament of reconciliation.

The Church describes the sacrament of reconciliation as a sacrament of:
- conversion, because it celebrates change in the life of the believer who turns back to God and away from sin;
- confession, because an essential element of the ritual encounter is the disclosing of sins;
- penance, because it celebrates one's steps in substituting healthy and holy actions in place of sin;
- forgiveness, because by it God's loving mercy is experienced;
- reconciliation, because it restores and reunites the sinner to God and to the Church. It heals relationships that have been severed or damaged by sin.

For This Week:

I want to remember:

I want to put my faith into action by:

Questions to Explore:

Prayer for the Week:

I confess to almighty God,
and to you, my brothers and sisters,
that I have sinned through my own fault
in my thoughts and in my words,
in what I have done,
and in what I have failed to do;
and I ask blessed Mary, ever virgin,
all the angels and saints,
and you, my brothers and sisters,
to pray for me to the Lord our God.

(The *Confiteor* from the Penitential Rite at Sunday Mass)

Twenty-sixth Sunday in Ordinary Time

Scripture:

Ezekiel 18:25-28
Psalm 125:4-5, 6-7, 8-9
Philippians 2:1-11
Matthew 21:28-32

Focus:

MORAL DECISION MAKING

Reflection:

Directions: In small groups, select one of the moral dilemmas presented below and discuss how you would make the moral choice based upon the goodness of the object, intention, and circumstances.

A. *Your teenage daughter, a senior in high school, is pregnant. She is a brilliant student, with a strong drive to follow a career in the medical profession. The father of the child is a freshman in college, pursuing a similar career. You and the boy's parents are average, middle-income families, who work outside the home to provide income for their costly education. How will you advise your child?*

B. *Your father was a drunk all his life. He abandoned your family when you were only two years old. Recently you heard that he was dying of cancer and wished to reconcile with you and your siblings. How will you choose?*

C. *You have struggled with trying to conceive a child for many years. Finally, through the wonders of medical science, you have had fertilized eggs implanted in your womb. During the first trimester, the doctors discover that four eggs have successfully been implanted. They advise that you sacrifice three to ensure the healthy development of one live birth. What will you decide?*

D. *Your ailing mother suffered for years with crippling arthritis. Now she is in a coma as a result of a massive stroke. She exists only on tubes and machines. You must make the decision to continue her life or pull the plug. How will you determine the moral good in this circumstance?*

E. *You are a single parent of three young children, supporting them by working the early morning shift as a nurse in a nearby hospital. The job is ideal, your neighbor helps you get them off to school in the morning, and you are home by the time they arrive in the late afternoon. The hospital where you are employed offers wonderful health benefits and a decent living wage. They are taken over by a large corporation and you discover that the new management will aggressively pursue clients who choose abortions, including late-term abortions. What will you do?*

Questions:

1. *How do the scriptures, the commandments of love, and the teachings of the Church provide a source of determining right from wrong in moral decision making?*

2. *What role does conscience play in your moral decision making?*

3. *How do your decisions have a ripple effect on the lives of others, even those you will never meet?*

Memorable People:

Sister Thea Bowman (1937-1990), a Franciscan, was a great witness to goodness in the American Catholic Church. She was of African-American descent and inspired not only her black brothers and sisters in the Church but others as well. She helped found the Institute of Black Catholic Studies at Xavier University in New Orleans and was widely traveled as a speaker and storyteller. In 1984, she was diagnosed with breast cancer and yet continued her teaching, preaching, and witnessing from her wheelchair, including a memorable witness talk given to the U.S. Conference of Catholic Bishops in 1989. She constantly called on her audiences to speak the Word that is Christ, the truth, and to act upon that Word. She once said, "Maybe I'm not making big changes in the world, but if I have somehow helped or encouraged somebody along the journey then I've done what I'm called to do" (*All Saints,* Robert Ellsberg, Crossroads Publishing Company, New York, 1997, p. 142). Sr. Thea Bowman died at the age of fifty-three.

The Church Says:

Catholics look to Jesus as their first teacher in how to live a moral life and in making decisions that are consonant with the good. In his earthly ministry and preaching and in his faithfulness to the kingdom of God unto death, Jesus provided for us an example of goodness. Throughout our lives we are faced with moral choices. We decide to tell the truth rather than lie, to be kind rather than cruel, to be fair rather than to cheat. At times, moral decisions can be complex and difficult, requiring a great deal of reflection. Then a process of reflection, prayer, listening to Church teaching, and seeking advice can help us to arrive at a good moral decision in accord with our conscience.

Traditional Catholic teaching emphasizes that the determination of the morality of a human act depends on three things: the object (the action itself, the thing which is done), the intention (the person's goal or purpose in doing the action), and the circumstances (particular features of individual situations in which an action is taken). Catholic moral theology holds that for an action to be judged as morally good, all three things (the object itself, the intention, and the circumstances) must be good (CCC 1755).

Conscience enables us to act responsibly. The Catholic perspective is that conscience is not an exercise in subjectivity—this "inner voice" must be informed, and Church teaching assists us in that formation. Through good preaching, sound religious education, an understanding of scripture, spiritual direction, the witness and example of other Christians, and the authoritative teaching of the Church, conscience is formed. It is a lifelong project where we prudently sift through our experience and the signs of the times, seek competent advice, and, with the help of the Holy Spirit, educate ourselves for the project of kingdom-living (CCC 1785).

For This Week:

I want to remember:

I want to put my faith into action by:

Questions to Explore:

Prayer for the Week:

*Spirit of God, you give us life when we choose
cooperation over competition;
forgiveness over revenge;
humility over conceit;
and love over hate.
Inspire us now to turn our lives around,
to follow the path of Christ,
putting on his attitudes and choosing God's will
over our own human weaknesses.
Give us wisdom as we confront the moral
dilemmas
that perplex and confuse us.
Help us as we surrender to your reign of justice,
joy, and peace.
Amen.*

Scripture:

Isaiah 5:1-7
Psalm 80:9, 12, 13-14, 15-16, 19-20
Philippians 4:6-9
Matthew 21:33-43

Focus:

DIVINE JUSTICE AND JUDGMENT

Reflection:

Directions: *Read through the following scenarios. Think about how justice would be applied to each situation from the human perspective. Then look over the same three circumstances and apply divine justice to the scenario. Write your responses in the space provided.*

> *Mark says he doesn't believe in a God. This world is all there is, so why not live it to the fullest. What difference does kindness or fairness or honesty make? After all, I'm in it for all that I can get. I plan to enjoy every minute of my life. Forget the rest of the world.*

Human justice:

Divine justice:

> *John had a difficult childhood. His grandmother looked out for him as best she could. John dropped out of school to get away from home. Struggling to keep alive, he would steal. Wages were never enough to pay the bills. John wanted more in life. One night, he was caught stealing and was shot as he tried to escape. As the paramedic was lifting John's stretcher into the ambulance, John mumbled, asking to be forgiven. He died before he arrived at the hospital.*

Human justice:

Divine justice:

> *Mary lived in a wealthy area of the city. She spent her time working for various humanitarian groups. She raised a great deal of money for the homeless shelters, yet she, herself, found it repulsive to spend time in the shelters. Mary hoped that people would not ask her to visit the shelters. She always found an excuse not to do so.*

Human justice:

Divine justice:

Questions:

1. *Describe what justice means to you.*

2. *Describe your understanding of God's justice.*

3. *In what ways are your understanding of justice and God's justice alike and different?*

Did You Know?

The practice of praying for the dead stems from an understanding of purgatory and that we can, by our prayers, intercede for those who are being purified and thus help them or assist them through these petitions.

Catholics frequently offer a donation for a Mass intention in memory of a loved one. The name of the deceased might be articulated near the end of the General Intercessions or the priest may have their name written on a card placed on the altar in order to remember them in a special way during the Mass. This practice varies from parish to parish. A "Mass card" is the card which records that such an intention will be remembered at Mass; it may be given as a gift.

The Church Says:

God created all things and desires all to be one, now and forever. God is just, always rejecting what is evil and embracing what is good. God is intimately aware of what we do and how it either draws us closer or pushes us away from the unity and goodness that God desires. God tolerates human sinfulness, which may seem unjust yet, by doing so, God gives everyone a full measure of time in which to repent. God's justice is eternal and surpasses all human judgments in its love and goodness.

God continually offers salvation to all. God did not abandon us after the fall from original grace. The Catholic Church teaches that no one is predestined to hell. Our vocation as human beings is, rather, in Jesus, our divinization and our complete union with God. Though the death and resurrection of Jesus reconciled us to God and overcame the reign of sin, nevertheless, sin still persists in the world. God created us in the image of God. We are most like God when in our freedom we choose goodness, right relationship with God and others, and live justly. However, we are also free to choose evil, which separates us from God.

For This Week:

I want to remember:

I want to put my faith into action by:

Questions to Explore:

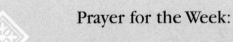

Prayer for the Week:

Take a favorite family album that contains pictures of deceased family and friends. As you thumb through the pages, spend a moment in quiet prayer for each person who has died. Voice your thanks to God for the gift that each one was to you. Conclude your prayer with:
Eternal rest grant unto them, O Lord, and let perpetual light shine upon them.

Twenty-eighth Sunday in Ordinary Time

Scripture:

Isaiah 25:6-10
Psalm 23:1-3, 3-4, 5, 6
Philippians 4:12-14, 19-20
Matthew 22:1-14
    [or (short form) 22:1-10]

Focus:

KEEP HOLY THE LORD'S DAY

Reflection:

Directions: *Write down your memories of Sunday celebrations and events and compare them to your activities on Sunday at this time in your life.*

Questions:

1. *What does the passage from Matthew's gospel reveal about the reign of God?*

2. *Describe the guests who received an invitation. Who might they be in today's world?*

3. *Describe the people of the byroads. Who might they be in today's world?*

Did You Know?

In addition to the worship that marks the Lord's Day, the actions of believers should characterize this day as a day of rest and leisure. Many Catholics also dedicate some time this day to charitable service of the sick and the elderly and other good works. Other Catholics also observe this as a day of reflection where the mind and spirit are cultivated, furthering Christian maturity and growth.

The Church Says:

Sunday is referred to as the Lord's Day, the eighth day, the first day of the week and, according to scripture, the day Jesus rose from the dead. On this day, Sunday, everything changed, in God, for the better. On the Lord's Day, Sunday, the Church celebrates the paschal mystery, the day the Lord rose from the dead. Thus, every Sunday is considered an Easter Day. On Sunday, the faithful are bound to come together in one place. The faithful come to listen to the Word of God and to take part in the Eucharist, which calls to mind the passion, resurrection, and the glory of the Lord Jesus and to give thanks to God that we, through baptism, are adopted sons and daughters and heirs to the kingdom prepared for us.

First and foremost, Sunday is kept holy by participating in the celebration of Mass. The precept (law) of the Church is that we are to participate in Mass on all Sundays and Holy Days of Obligation except in cases of illness or care of infants and the sick. Sunday is to be observed as the Lord's Day; thus, it is hoped that it may become a day of joy and freedom from work. No other celebrations are to take precedence over Sunday, unless they are of great importance, such as Christmas.

Sunday is the day when believers gather in one place to raise their minds, their hearts, and their voices in praise of God who has made them one, uniting them in the sacrifice of Jesus. Sunday, the Lord's Day, is the festival day when our passover in Christ from death and sin to new life and grace is celebrated. For us believers it is a markedly communal day; a day when we draw together with one voice and heart to praise the Son who has risen in our lives and illumines us with truth, beauty, and love.

For This Week:

I want to remember:

I want to put my faith into action by:

Questions to Explore:

Prayer for the Week:

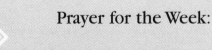

You, Lord, are my shepherd;
I do not lack for anything.
In green pastures you give me rest;
beside quiet streams you lead me;
you refresh my spirit.

You direct my path to do your will.
Though I am in darkness I am not afraid;
for you are always with me.
You protect me.
You give me courage.

You set a table for me
even in sight of my enemies;
you have called me and I am yours.
All that is good and kind surrounds me
each and every day.
I look to the day when I will dwell in your
house forever and ever. Amen.
(Paraphrase of Psalm 23)

Twenty-ninth Sunday in Ordinary Time

Scripture:

Isaiah 45:1, 4-6
Psalm 96:1, 3, 4-5, 7-8, 9-10
1 Thessalonians 1:1-5
Matthew 22:15-21

Focus:

"I Am The Lord, There Is No Other"

Reflection:

Directions: In the space below write down several things that occupy your time and mind each day. After listing your concerns, think about the one God who creates, favors, and loves us. Write a poem, a paragraph, or a psalm indicating your belief in the one God who is Lord of your life and of the entire universe.

Questions:

1. *What internal changes are needed to place God first in your life?*

2. *How do your daily concerns fade in the light of God's power and creative love?*

3. *What response can you make to the Lord of all?*

Memorable People:

Lydia, a business woman who traded in precious purple cloth, was the first European convert to Christianity. After her baptism and the conversion of her entire household, she opened her home to the missionaries Paul and Silas, saying, "If you consider me a believer in the Lord, come and stay at my home." She is an example of an early Christian leader who put her faith in the Lord into action.

Did You Know?

St. Cyril of Jerusalem (d. 386), bishop during the difficult years of the Arian heresy, helped to promote pilgrimages to the Holy Land. His primary surviving work is a collection of catechesis, instructions to catechumens preparing for baptism. In it, he writes, "Seeing then that many have gone astray in divers ways from the One God, some having deified the sun . . . others the moon . . . others the other parts of the world; others the arts; others their various kinds of food; others their pleasures . . . and others dazzled by the brightness of gold have deified it and the other kinds of matter—whereas if one lay as a first foundation in [one's] heart the doctrine of the unity of God, and trust to Him, [one] roots out at once the whole crop of the evils of idolatry . . . lay thou, therefore, this first doctrine of religion as a foundation in thy soul by faith" (St. Cyril of Jerusalem, Catechetical Instructions, On the Ten Points of Doctrine, found in *The Heart of Catholicism*, Theodore E. James, ed., Our Sunday Visitor, Inc., Huntington, Indiana, 1997, p. 181).

The Church Says:

Catholics believe that, according to divine revelation, God is shown to be a loving God who has created the human race and brought us out of bondage. The people chosen as God's own were constituted as a people by divine favor and, as an outstanding mark of God's love and power, were freed from slavery in Egypt (Exodus 20:2-5). The covenant God who liberated these, our spiritual forebears, from slavery demanded acceptance and service and worship from his people (Matthew 4:10). The first of the Ten Commandments, therefore, most fittingly concerns the unique loyalty that is due to God from the chosen people: "[Y]ou shall have no other gods before me." (Exodus 20:3).

In the fullness of time, a new covenant in Jesus was established. Christ's teaching that we sum up all our obligations and duties toward God by loving the Most High with our whole heart, soul, and mind (Matthew 22:37) echoes the great prayer and call of faith of the first covenant, "Hear, O Israel: the Lord our God is one Lord" (Deuteronomy 6:4). Based in the scriptural witness of both the Old and New Testament and based in our own experience and witness as a Church, we affirm that there are no other gods. There is only one God, the creator and redeemer, and to that God alone is given our service and worship (CCC 2084).

Our Catholic faith also attests that the God in whom we place our trust is constant and unchanging. God, who is perfect, remains always the same, always faithful, always just and without evil. Given such perfection, it is clearly a privilege to follow and accept the covenant relationship of mercy and goodness that God offers us in Jesus. Indeed, the question becomes, Who would want to reject or not follow such a God? (CCC 2086)

For This Week:

I want to remember:

I want to put my faith into action by:

Questions to Explore:

Prayer for the Week:

God, you are our God.
You alone rule the heavens and the rhythms of nature.
You, Lord, are the one God, manifested in three
  persons,
    Father, Jesus and Holy Spirit.
Your dominion covers the face of the earth
  and all the wondrous marvels of the universe.
We cannot grasp the breath and depth of your power
  and your loving care.
Open our minds that we might believe in you more
  fully.
Mold us that we might place our hope in you,
  even in difficult times.
Melt our hearts that we might love all that you have
  created.
In the name of Jesus who has redeemed us, we pray.
Amen.

Thirtieth Sunday in Ordinary Time

Scripture:

Exodus 22:20-26
Psalm 18:2-3, 3-4, 47, 51
1 Thessalonians 1:5-10
Matthew 22:34-40

Focus:

THE TWO
GREAT COMMANDMENTS

Reflection:

Directions: *In the space below indicate several ordinary ways you can better model God's compassion and love, by loving your neighbor and yourself.*

Questions:

1. *Why is Christian love so countercultural in our society?*

2. *What ways does this community of faith support you in the difficult changes that are implied by love of God and neighbor?*

3. *What is it that connects you to others, making humankind interdependent?*

Quotable Quotes:

" 'You shall love the Lord your God with all your heart, and with
all your soul, and with all your mind.' This is the greatest and first commandment.
And a second is like it: 'You shall love your neighbor as yourself.'
On these two commandments hang all the law and the prophets."
(Matthew 22:37-40)

Memorable People:

Dorothy Day (1897-1980) was cofounder along with Peter Maurin (1877-1949) of the Catholic Worker movement that promotes a gospel critique of society based on the message that we see Christ in our neighbors. Day opened the offices of the Catholic Worker as a "house of hospitality," offering food and shelter for those displaced by the Great Depression. This was one of many such houses. Day spoke of her being thrilled as a little girl reading about the lives of the saints, but she said, "I could see the nobility of giving one's life for the sick, the maimed, the leper. . . . But there was another question in my mind. Why was so much done in remedying the evil instead of avoiding it in the first place. . . . Where were the saints to try to change the social order, not just to minister to the slaves, but to do away with slavery?" (Dorothy Day quoted in *All Saints*, Robert Ellsberg, Crossroad Publishing Company, New York, 1997, p. 519).

The Church Says:

The bishops who met at the Second Vatican Council noted, "Love of God and of one's neighbor, then, is the first and greatest commandment. . . . It goes without saying that this is a matter of the utmost importance to [humankind] who are coming to rely more and more on each other and to a world which is becoming more unified every day" (GS 24).

The unity which characterizes God the Father, the Son, and the Holy Spirit is the impetus for mutual reliance and unity among peoples. The Church affirms the gospel truth that love of God and neighbor cannot be separated. She offers these characteristics or principles implied in acting out of love for God and neighbor in these terms: interdependence, the common good, respect of the human person, solidarity, and the requirements of peace and justice. Interdependence is a requirement of our human nature and the medium by which individuals respond to their calling from God. The Church teaches that every group that composes society must take into account and acknowledge the needs and legitimate aspirations of every other group. Respect for the human person, actualized in giving every person access to the basics in life, is a necessary component of a society that has the common good as its focus.

Jesus saves us and creates for us a Church whereby we experience the depths of our communion with God and one another. Church communities that render mutual sacrifice increase the solidarity of the faithful members and bring to fulfillment the kingdom of God. Catholics have a concrete responsibility for one another's welfare. Each generation must provide the next with reasons for life and optimism.

For This Week:

I want to remember:

I want to put my faith into action by:

Questions to Explore:

Prayer for the Week:

God of compassion and love,
your covenant of love compels us
to love our neighbor
with the same kindness and mercy
which you generously lavish upon us.
Yet we are blind to the stranger and alien,
we forget the widow and orphan,
and we hold tight our possessions and gifts.
Open wide our stiff hearts and heal our blindness.
We pray that we might learn to love you and our
neighbor
with a wholehearted commitment and strength,
knowing that you first chose and loved us.
We ask this in our loving Savior, Jesus,
under the power of the Holy Spirit.
Amen.

Thirty-first Sunday in Ordinary Time

Scripture:

Malachi 1:14–2:2, 8-10
Psalm 131:1, 2, 3
1 Thessalonians 2:7-9, 13
Matthew 23:1-12

Focus:

THE ROLE OF THE MAGISTERIUM

Reflection:

Directions: *Think about the qualities that you expect to find in a leader. Base your notions on the scriptures for this week and list them here. Take a few minutes to name people or events that have exemplified these qualities.*

Questions:

1. *Name insights and clarifications you have gained regarding the role of the magisterium of the Church.*

2. *What confidence do you find in the way the Church is organized?*

3. *What issues does this raise for you?*

Quotable Quotes:

Three months after his election as pope, John XXIII called for an ecumenical council of the Church whose goal would be an updating, or, in Italian, *aggiornamento*. John XXIII said, "The substance of the ancient deposit of faith is one thing, and the way in which it is presented is another."

Did You Know?

The Church's interpretation of scripture helps us to understand that while all scripture contains religious truth, some statements are not to be taken literally. Rather, their point or message is to be grasped. For example, why is the priest called "Father" when the scripture says that no one is to be called father "but God in heaven"? First, recall that we do call our biological father by the name "father." Our human fathers are our first teachers and examples and are rightfully called by that term of respect. The Church uses the honorific title "father" for priests and abbots similarly, to indicate their role in leading people to God. The point of the scriptural injunction to "call no man father" is that no one, regardless of title, may supplant God's primary place in our lives. This we firmly believe and uphold.

114

The Church Says:

As St. Paul claims to teach with authority, it is an authority which ultimately rests on the source of his teachings, and Paul makes it clear that those teachings are of divine, not human, origin. Catholic belief holds that bishops are the successors of the apostles and that they are blessed with the authority of Jesus Christ, authentically teaching, informing the faith of people and directing their conduct. In other words, we believe that those who exercise teaching authority in the Church are sent by Christ. They do not create the gospel but are gifted by the sacrament of ordination to be Christ's emissaries. This is often referred to as the magisterium of the Church. The magisterium is challenged to serve the Word of God; teaching that which has been handed on to us, leading the faithful with the help of the Holy Spirit. The role of the Holy Spirit is to direct and guide the magisterium.

The Catholic Church upholds that there are various levels of articulating the teachings. We believe that God guarantees the possibility of objectively professing belief without error. The Holy Spirit's presence in and through the leaders is the guarantor. The pope exercises the gift of infallibility when he proclaims by a definitive act a doctrine pertaining to faith and morals.

Without magisterial authority, the Church could never propose that the faith be articulated in a particular way at certain points in history. In other words, we could never as a community objectively grapple with what has been revealed to us by God. The Church would not be able to adequately preach the gospel, apply it to life, or formulate creeds. The role of the magisterium is to provide surety, in Christ, of the expression of faith and how that faith is put into practice.

For This Week:

I want to remember:

I want to put my faith into action by:

Questions to Explore:

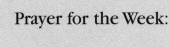

Prayer for the Week:

God, you are our teacher.
You guide and direct us
through the Holy Spirit.
Keep all leaders open
to the direction and guidance of your Spirit.
Help them to keep focused
on the truth of your word
so that deeds and words are synonymous.
Help us to do the same.
We ask this in Jesus' name.
Amen.

Thirty-second Sunday in Ordinary Time

Scripture:

Wisdom 6:12–16
Psalm 63:2, 3–4, 5–6, 7–8
1 Thessalonians 4:13–18 or 4:13–14
Matthew 25:1–13

Focus:

PERSEVERANCE
IN PRAYER

Reflection:

Directions: *Recall an experience that required waiting for someone or something to which you committed yourself to wait. Describe the experience. Articulate your ability to wait and to be committed to waiting. What does it require of you? How do you respond when the wait is finished?*

Questions:

Complete the following:

A person who has helped me to pray is . . .

My first remembrance of praying is . . .

My time and place to pray is . . .

I would describe prayer as . . .

When it appears my prayers go unanswered I . . .

I feel I can't pray when . . .

What challenges me most in my prayer is . . .

Did You Know?

Catholics use various postures in praying.
Kneeling expresses our inferior relationship to the Most High who has created and redeemed us.
Standing indicates our dignity before God as creatures created in God's own image.
Palms outstretched before the Almighty symbolize that we have nothing of worth to offer but ourselves. It may also indicate receptivity to a gift from God.
Prostration is a sign acknowledging God as supreme, that we can do nothing without the divine presence and are totally open to the animating Spirit.
Standing, kneeling, or *lying prostrate with arms stretched out in the form of a cross* symbolizes our total reliance on the loving self-sacrifice of Jesus, embracing in faith that total abandonment of self in obedience to God's will.

The Church Says:

Prayer is the link between God and ourselves. Prayer is also a gift, which is sustained by the Holy Spirit. Our desire to pray can be sidelined by numerous distractions. Sometimes in our desire to rid ourselves of these distractions, we fall deeper into them and are unable to pray at all. The best remedy for distractions is to turn further into the depths of one's heart, for there, in the most intimate place, is where God speaks to us.

Another difficulty that our Catholic tradition warns in the life of prayer is inner dryness. This type of barrenness is described as the experience where nothing "works" in prayer, where the person praying feels separated from God. Neither in one's thoughts, nor in one's memories, nor in one's feelings is there any inkling of God's intimate presence. This lack of presence prompts one to ask where God is. This experience is the penultimate moment of faith. Even Jesus experienced such an episode in his agony in the garden. It is the experience of the tomb where the Lord was laid to rest. It requires the faithful heart throwing itself totally upon the God of conversion, who alone will vindicate and transform it.

In the Catholic tradition, prayer is not manipulation of God. It is an expression of our mutual thirst, God for us and us for God. It is a form of vigilance against the darkness and evil of the world. Prayer is the self-expression of a heart attitude attuned to the love of the divine, responding to that gift of heaven, not from the height of pride but from the depth, the font of humility. Prayer is our communion with the one who has made life possible for us in Christ.

For This Week:

I want to remember:

I want to put my faith into action by:

Questions to Explore:

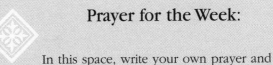

Prayer for the Week:

In this space, write your own prayer and pray it each day this week.

Thirty-third Sunday in Ordinary Time

Scripture:

Proverbs 31:10-13, 19-20, 30-31
Psalm 128:1-2, 3, 4-5
1 Thessalonians 5:1-6
Matthew 25:14-30

Focus:

STEWARDSHIP

Reflection:

Directions: *Use the space below to write about your experience with the wise one. Include the qualities of a wise person that you wish to emulate. Close the description with a short prayer of gratitude to Jesus, who is Wisdom.*

Questions:

1. *In the light of the parable of the silver pieces and the gospel implications of stewardship, how are we challenged to be wise stewards of this earth and its inhabitants?*

2. *Name some practical ways that disciples of Jesus today can care for God's creation and the peoples of the earth.*

3. *As you hear the Church's teaching on stewardship, what is evoked in you?*

Memorable People:

St. Francis of Assisi wrote hymns of praise to "brother sun and sister moon." St. Francis and St. Philip Neri both were known for the kind way in which they treated animals, seeing in them the praise of God, their Creator.

Did You Know?

The *Roman Ritual*, in its Book of Blessings, contains many prayers for acknowledging the importance of (and blessing) such things as an office, shop, or factory, centers for social communication, a gym or athletic field, boats and fishing gear, technical installations or equipment, tools for work, fields, flocks, seeds, and animals. Many of the prayers express the beauty of creation and humanity's role in preserving and protecting what God has given us. For example, the Church prays in blessing tools for work, "In your loving providence, O God, you have made the forces of nature subject to the work of our hands. Grant that by devotion to our own work we may gladly cooperate with you in the building up of creation" (BB 935).

The Church Says:

Jesus provides us with a model for wise Christian stewardship in his life and ministry, giving totally of himself to effect our wholeness and communion with God. The root of this word is the Anglo-Saxon term *stigweard* or "hall keeper," implying the person responsible for feeding the entire manor. When we connect this term to the Greek word in scripture, *oikonomos,* or "household manager," we uncover the deeper sense of the Christian term "stewardship." *Oikos* refers to household and all relations. Thus, the gospel sense of stewardship implies the care and wise management of the entire household of God—all of creation, particularly humankind.

Love of God and neighbor requires that we use our time, gifts, and resources to help others, particularly by reversing the exploitation of the vulnerable members of our society, and practicing the corporal works of mercy, namely, feeding the hungry, clothing the naked, housing the homeless, caring for the sick, and visiting the imprisoned. Because God has fashioned us out of unity, we are interdependent with one another and the entire created universe. Thus, a wise steward works to change systems to alleviate the enormity of human misery. Reverence for the Creator calls us to respect the earth and nature, and to value and work to preserve the vitality of our planet. Ecological attitudes and practices and the valuing of work as an act of co-creation are implicit in the goodness of creation. Finally, our attitudes toward possessions, particularly that of owning property, must be infused with principles that promote harmony, wholeness, and generosity in building toward the fulfillment of God's kingdom.

For This Week:

I want to remember:

I want to put my faith into action by:

Questions to Explore:

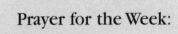

Prayer for the Week:

God of this vast universe, who are we that you love us so? You have created us in your image and likeness, empowering us to experience wonder and joy at the goodness of all of life. Each day the beauty of your wonderful world surrounds us. Give us the eyes to see your marvelous works, the ears to hear the music of life, and the conviction to respond to the needs of others. Give us generous and thankful hearts, that we might share all our blessings to build your kingdom here and now. We want to live in the blessed assurance that Christ will come again to embrace us and reward our care for your creation. Empower us in the living Spirit breathed into us from creation's dawn. Amen.

Thirty-fourth Sunday in Ordinary Time

Scripture:

Ezekiel 34:11-12, 15-17
Psalm 23:1-2, 2-3, 5-6
1 Corinthians 15:20-26, 28
Matthew 25:31-46

Focus:

"TO JUDGE THE LIVING AND THE DEAD"

Reflection:

Directions: *In the space provided, write your description of Christ the King. Follow this with your written commitment to Christ, consecrating yourself to live and act following the kingdom imperative to love your neighbor and your God. Use the images from the final judgment in Matthew's gospel as a guide to articulate your commitment to Christ the King.*

Questions:

1. *As you think about how you will be judged, what changes in lifestyle do you desire?*

2. *How would you describe the reign of Christ the King, here, but not yet fully revealed?*

3. *What hopes do you have as a result of this session?*

Quotable Quotes:

On this feast of Christ the King, the Church prays, "As king [Christ] claims dominion over all creation, that he may present to you, his heavenly Father, an eternal and universal kingdom: a kingdom of truth and life, a kingdom of holiness and grace, a kingdom of justice, love and peace" (*Sacramentary,* Preface 51).

Did You Know?

The anchor was one of the most popular early Christian symbols connected to Christ, and use of it refers to Hebrews 6:18-19. It is seen on early Christian graves and seals and was recommended by Clement of Alexandria (c. 200) as an image suitable for use in seal rings. The crossbar of the anchor also was understood as a symbol of Christ's cross. Sometimes artisans depicted dolphins twined around the anchor (perhaps a sign of humanity's being saved from drowning in the seas of sin by Christ?). Some modern Catholic medals shaped as anchors are also inscribed with names of the theological virtues of faith, hope, and charity—those virtues from God that form our lives as believers and thus 'anchor' us.

The Church Says:

In Christ all of human history is summed up and fulfilled. Christ the King is the key, center, and purpose of the whole of human history. His kingdom is here, but not yet fully revealed. While the cross defeated evil, it continues to resist Christ's reign. The final fulfillment, a new heaven and a new earth in which justice dwells, will be accomplished, for we are in the final age of the world. As Paul says in Romans 8:22–23, "We know that the whole creation has been groaning in labor pains until now; and not only the creation, but we ourselves, who have the first fruits of the Spirit, groan inwardly while we wait for adoption, the redemption of our bodies."

Christ the King will judge the living and the dead. The Church teaches that there are two judgments. The first, called particular judgment, is the judging of the moral quality of one's life immediately after death, when Christ determines whether the person has fundamentally chosen to cooperate with God's grace or to reject it. Final judgment refers to the endtime in history when Christ will come again bringing the fullness of his kingdom and sum up everything by passing definitive judgment on all people, nations, and history itself. In the light of the gospel message, Christ judges each according to how he or she lived in accord with the kingdom imperative to love one's neighbor, thus expressing wholehearted love for God. At the last judgment, Christ the living Word will reveal God's glorious triumph over evil and at the same time manifest the ultimate meaning of the whole work of creation. Until that time we pass through trial and faith-shaking events, holding firm to the Lord of hope.

For This Week:

I want to remember:

I want to put my faith into action by:

Questions to Explore:

Prayer for the Week:

Christ, our shepherd king,
rescue us from sin and heal our wounds.
You are the first fruits of the living sacrifice
made to God.
Consecrate us to your saving work.
Instruct and guide us as we journey in faith
and love.
Let your coming in glory at the end of time
be a time of rejoicing for each of us,
as we strive to live out your command of
love in this life.
Amen.

HOLY DAYS AND FEASTS

The Immaculate Conception

Scripture:

Genesis 3:9-15, 20
Psalm 98:1, 2-3, 3-4
Ephesians 1:3-6, 11-12
Luke 1:26-38

Focus:

IMMACULATE CONCEPTION OF MARY

Reflection:

Directions: *In the space below are the opening lines from today's gospel. Read these prayerfully, and then use your imagination to write your description of Mary, favored daughter of God and wholly integrated (sinless) woman. You may choose to write in the form of a poem, a symbolic story (like the story of Adam and Eve), or a short scene from a movie or play.*

"Rejoice, O highly favored daughter! The Lord is with you." "Blessed are you among women." "Do not fear, Mary. You have found favor with God."

Questions:

1. *How has God's grace overcome sin in your personal experiences?*

2. *What can you learn from these stories of Eve and Mary?*

3. *What does this doctrine of the Immaculate Conception of Mary awaken in you?*

Quotable Quotes:

Pope Paul VI stipulates Guidelines for Devotion to the Blessed Virgin Mary (1974), saying, "The ultimate purpose of devotion to the Blessed Virgin is to glorify God and lead Christians to commit themselves to a life which conforms absolutely to his will."

Did You Know?

In 1846, the bishops of the United States chose Mary under the title of the Immaculate Conception to be the patroness of this relatively new country. Soon after that, the building of a shrine in her honor in Washington, D.C., was begun. This shrine, called the National Shrine of the Immaculate Conception, is located at the edge of the campus of the Catholic University of America.

The Church Says:

Today's feast celebrates that from the moment of her conception in the womb of Anne, Mary was free from original sin and all its effects. This special grace from God flows out of Mary's role in God's plan for the salvation of humankind. The doctrine of the Immaculate Conception is not found in scripture. However, since the earliest days of the Church, the belief that Mary was free from the stain of original sin has been upheld. Pope Pius IX declared the doctrine of Mary's Immaculate Conception an infallible dogma on December 8, 1854. This favor bestowed upon Mary is not a result of something she did but is the action of God upon her. This is also true in our lives. Everything depends on gift—grace from God.

Mary's "yes" to the invitation to become the mother of God gives her an esteemed place in salvation history and provides for us a model of a true disciple, that is, conformity to God's will. The breach with God described in the Genesis account of Adam and Eve disobeying God's command has been made whole through the obedient submission of Mary to God's plan for the salvation of humanity.

For This Week:

I want to remember:

I want to put my faith into action by:

Questions to Explore:

Prayer for the Week:

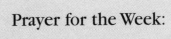

Loving and gracious God,
we thank and praise you on this day
for the gift of Mary, your Mother.
You honored this simple woman
with the favor of sinlessness.
You gave Mary the privilege of conceiving
and bearing your beloved Son.
Her "yes" to the angel's announcement
opened the way for our salvation.

O Mary, conceived without sin,
pray that we too might respond
in faithfulness and love to God,
and thus also bear Christ
in today's world. Amen.

The Solemnity of Mary, Mother of God

Scripture:

Numbers 6:22-27
Psalm 67:2-3, 5, 6, 8
Galatians 4:4-7
Luke 2:16-21

Focus:

THEOTOKOS

Reflection:

Directions: *From the gospel and the teaching on Mary, Mother of God, write down three to five characteristics or qualities evident in Mary. When you have finished, choose the quality you believe God is inviting you to manifest in your own life. Write a short, concrete description of how you could incorporate that quality in your own life.*

Qualities of Mary:

In my life . . .

Questions:

1. *What experience of Christ in your life do you treasure in your heart?*

2. *How does Mary, Mother of God, known as Theotokos, influence your life?*

Quotable Quotes:

" *Mary treasured all these words and pondered them in her heart.* "
(Luke 2:19)

Did You Know?

Federico Barocci (1575-79) captures Mary, the Mother of God, in one of her aspects as universal mother. In his painting entitled "Madonna del Popolo" (Mother of the People), the Virgin intercedes for us. She is being blessed by Christ in the heavens, supported by cherubs under which is a dove, representing the Holy Spirit. The dove hovers over a crowd of adults and children, both rich and poor. A wealthy mother points to the apparition of Christ and Mary, but her young children are more interested in the byplay between a beggar and a street musician. The whole piece is full of movement and life, including Mary's loving gaze upon her Son and the motion of her hands as they present to him the people below. (HistItal 657)

The Church Says:

During this Christmas season, the Church celebrates this feast of Mary because of her role in Christ's birth. The Church proclaimed that Mary is truly the Mother of God at the Council of Ephesus in 431. The Greek word used for this feast, *theotokos,* means one who has given birth to God. Jesus is truly human and divine, one person with two natures. The Church arrived at the truth that for Mary to be the Mother of Jesus means that she is the mother of God as well as the mother of Jesus in his humanity. Mary is inseparably linked with the saving work of her Son. The Church honors Mary because she freely cooperated in the work of our salvation through her faith and obedience.

For This Week:

I want to remember:

I want to put my faith into action by:

Questions to Explore:

Prayer for the Week:

God, you are the source of light in the world.
You have sent your Son, Jesus,
to dwell among your people
through the womb of Mary, your Mother.
Marvelous are your works, O God!
Mary, through her faithful love,
gave birth to the Savior,
called Wonderful God, Prince of Peace.
We ask that Mary's fidelity,
born of a humble heart,
encourage us to bear your light and peace
in our world.
We ask this through Christ,
your Word made flesh.
Amen.

The Presentation of the Lord

Scripture:

Malachi 3:1-4
Psalm 24:7, 8, 9, 10
Hebrews 2:14-18
Luke 2:22-40

Focus:

THE TWO NATURES

Reflection:

Directions: *As you listen to the gospel from Luke 2:22-40, place yourself in the position of Simeon, Anna, and Jesus' parents. Then in the three columns below indicate what each of these characters in the account reveals to you about the nature of Jesus.*

SIMEON   ANNA   MARY and JOSEPH

Questions:

1. *What about the nature of Jesus has been revealed to you through the people and the circumstances of your life?*

2. *In the light of the observations of these holy people and your own experience, who is Jesus?*

Did You Know?

In the northern hemisphere this feast is celebrated in the dead of winter darkness. The assembly gathers prior to the liturgy outside the church and candles are blessed. As these blessed candles are lit, the people process into church singing and the Mass of the Presentation of the Lord is celebrated. Customarily, enough candles are blessed on this day in order to last through the year. Thus, this feast also goes by the name "Candlemas."

The Church Says:

The Catholic Church confesses belief in Jesus, the second person of the Trinity, as possessing two natures. That is, Jesus Christ is fully human and fully divine. While this is based in the apostles' experience of him and is asserted by scripture, the theological understanding of this doctrine was first addressed by the Council of Chalcedon in 451 due to the Monophysite controversy (or heresy). The Monophysites charged that the human nature of Christ ceased to exist when the divine person of the Son of God assumed it.

The Council of Chalcedon proclaimed, "Following the holy Father, we unanimously teach and confess one and the same Son, our Lord Jesus Christ: the same perfect in divinity and perfect in humanity, the same truly God and truly man, composed of rational soul and body; consubstantial with the Father as to his divinity and consubstantial with us as to his humanity; 'like us in all things but sin.'" The Council then answered the Monophysites and asserted, "We confess that one and the same Christ . . . is to be acknowledged in two natures without confusion, change, division, or separation. The distinction between the natures was never abolished by their union, but rather the character proper to each of the two natures was preserved as they came together in one person . . ." (Council of Chalcedon, DS 301-02)

Another way the Church expresses this is to assert that Jesus is both the Son of God and the Son of the Virgin Mary. The two natures of Christ, one divine and one human, are not confused, but united. They are united in the one person of Jesus Christ. This union does not cease.

For This Week:

I want to remember:

I want to put my faith into action by:

Questions to Explore:

Prayer for the Week:

Jesus, we desire to be messengers of your Good News. There are many in this world who need to hear the message of your human and divine presence with us. In your humanity, you have walked with us, felt the pains and joys of living, and have loved much. In your divinity, you are our source of sustenance and transformation. We raise up to you not only ourselves, but those whose names be presented to this circle of prayer. You, who promised to be with us as we gather, have heard our cry. Give us the courage to share all that you have come to mean in our lives. Give us the words to speak the glory of your presence and promise—Son of God and Child of Mary. Prepare the hearts of those we bring before you that they might hear all that you have accomplished in your living, dying, and rising. Amen.

The Ascension of the Lord

Scripture:

Acts 1:1v11
Psalm 47:2–3, 6–7, 8–9
Ephesians 1:17–23
Matthew 28:16–20

Focus:

THE ASCENSION OF THE LORD

Questions:

1. *What do you feel as you picture Jesus ascending to heaven?*

2. *What does the ascension mean for you?*

Quotable Quotes:

"Jesus Christ . . . has gone into heaven and is at the right hand of God, with angels, authorities, and powers made subject to him." (1 Peter 3:22)

"He was lifted up, and a cloud took him out of their sight . . . Why do you stand looking up toward heaven? This Jesus, who has been taken up from you into heaven, will come in the same way as you saw him go into heaven." (Acts of the Apostles 1:9, 11)

Did You Know?

The feast of the Ascension was celebrated from the later years of the fourth century. The celebration in the early years included a procession to the Mount of Olives, where the ascension is said to have occurred.

The Church Says:

The Risen Christ, forty days after the resurrection, ascended into heaven. The ascension was witnessed by the apostles. The ascension closes the post-resurrection appearances. Christ left this world in bodily form so that the Spirit that was promised could come. Christ ascended by his own power into heaven. In a new way the work of the Church was begun, to be empowered by the Spirit on Pentecost. Christ's time on earth in physical form began with Mary's agreement to become his mother, and ended with the ascension. The Church symbolically views Jesus as sitting in majesty at God's right hand. The Church awaits the second coming of Christ, when all of human history will be brought under his authority.

For This Week:

I want to remember:

I want to put my faith into action by:

Questions to Explore:

Prayer for the Week:

Lord Jesus,
*   you ascended in glory.*
You are my hope.
May I follow you into the new creation.
Until that time may I have the joy
*   of experiencing your presence with me*
*   as you promised.*
Amen.

Trinity Sunday

Scripture:

Exodus 34:4–6, 8–9
Daniel 3:52–56
2 Corinthians 13:11–13
John 3:16–18

Focus:

THE HOLY TRINITY

Reflection:

Directions: *The Bible gives many of the three persons of the Trinity. Brainstorm events of the Bible referring to the three persons and list them below. When you have finished, list the various qualities and names you associate with each person of the Trinity.*

GOD, CREATOR, YAHWEH	JESUS	HOLY SPIRIT

Scripture

References

Qualities

Names

Quotable Quotes:

The traditional Catholic hymn, "Holy God, We Praise Thy Name" (ascribed to Ignaz Franz, [d. 1790] and translated into English by Clarence Walworth [d. 1900]), has as its closing verse an acknowledgment of the Trinity: "Holy Father, Holy Son,/ Holy Spirit, Three we name thee,/ While in essence only One,/ Undivided God we claim thee,/ And adoring bend the knee,/ While we own the mystery."

Did You Know?

In Christian iconography, the Trinity is symbolized by a triangle (the Greek letter "delta"). In early Byzantine art, God the Father is not portrayed by a human figure, but rather the *dextera Domini*, the hand of God, as in the apse of St. Mark Cathedral (Venice), dating from the ninth century. Later, in western art, the Trinity is portrayed using human figures, such as in the manuscript miniatures of Jean Fouquet (d. 1481), one of the foremost French artists of his day. In the Hours of Etienne Chevalier, dating from 1470, he (Chantilly) represents the Trinity as three identical figures seated on identical thrones. This type of representation of the Trinity, employing human figures, is said to have been banned by Pope Urban VIII because the Holy Spirit was to be illustrated through the use of a dove or tongues of fire.

The Church Says:

The doctrine of the Trinity, three persons in one God, is the central mystery of the Christian faith because it is the mystery of God's very self. Christian faith is founded on belief in the Trinity. Baptism is done "in the name of the Father, and of the Son, and of the Holy Spirit."

The doctrine of the Trinity is found in the Apostles' Creed, and again in the Nicene Creed formulated in 325. This creed states the belief in a God of three equal persons, who have no beginning or end. This belief arises out of and expresses a continuing human experience of God as Father, Son, and Spirit. From the time of Jesus the Spirit is further identified as the Spirit of Jesus and continues the mission of Jesus to bring about the reign of God in the world.

The Church expresses this threefold experience of God in the baptismal formula, in scripture (for example, 2 Corinthians 13:13 and Ephesians 4:4-6), in preaching, catechesis, and the prayer of the Church. We begin Mass and many other prayers as we are baptized "in the name of the Father, and of the Son, and of the Holy Spirit." The Sacramentary addresses prayers to God that conclude with "We ask this through our Lord Jesus Christ, your Son, who lives and reigns with you and the Holy Spirit, one God, for ever and ever."

The words "substance," "essence," and "nature" indicate the oneness of God. The term "person" designates the three, Father, Son, and Spirit, who are distinct. The word "relation" indicates that their distinction lies in the relationship of each to the others.

For This Week:

I want to remember:

I want to put my faith into action by:

Questions to Explore:

Prayer for the Week:

In the name of the Father, and of the Son,
and of the Holy Spirit.
You are kind, compassionate,
and slow to anger.
I praise you, who are Creator,
Savior, and Spirit of peace and love.
Teach my heart to recognize you
in your creative energy,
in dying and rising,
and in your powerful and gentle
movements.
May I know your love in the love I experience
and share with my sisters and brothers.
Amen.

The Body and Blood of Christ

Scripture:

Deuteronomy 8:2-3, 14-16
Psalm 147:12-13, 14-15, 19-20
1 Corinthians 10:16-17
John 6:51-58

Focus:

THE REAL PRESENCE

Reflection:

Directions: *As you grapple with the words of Paul to the Corinthians and the gospel passage from John, reflect on the words of Jesus and Paul listed below. Then begin to write about the implications of this passage for you and the People of God. For example, as we unite ourselves with Jesus, what implication does that have on our relationships with others in the human family?*

I am the living bread

Anyone who eats this bread shall live forever

The bread I give is my flesh

If you do not eat the flesh of the Son of Man and drink his blood, you have no life in you

My flesh is real food

My blood is real drink

Whoever feeds on my flesh and drinks my blood remains in me and I in him [her]

The cup of blessing is a sharing in the blood of Christ

The bread we share is a sharing in the body of Christ

Because the loaf is one, we, though many, are one body

Questions:

1. *Why does the Church continue to celebrate the sacrament of Eucharist?*

2. *How would you describe the change that takes place in the elements of bread and wine?*

3. *What do you believe about Eucharist, the real presence of Christ?*

Did You Know?

For the first six centuries of the Church's life, communion was routinely offered to all the faithful under the forms of bread and wine. During the Middle Ages, however, the practice of sharing the chalice with the laity gradually died out. In response to challenges from the Protestant reformers in the sixteenth century, the Council of Trent affirmed the practice of sharing the consecrated bread alone. In our own century, however, the Second Vatican Council restored the ancient practice of offering communion under both forms to the laity, so that, in the words of Pope Paul VI, "a fuller light" would shine on the eucharistic banquet.

The Catholic tradition has always maintained the use of a common cup in communion, in order to emphasize the communal nature of our eucharistic sharing. Whether each person takes the cup and drinks from it, or the consecrated bread is dipped in the consecrated wine (intinction), or, as in the Eastern rite Catholic Churches, the consecrated bread is soaked in the consecrated wine and placed in the mouth with a spoon, all employ a common cup.

The Church Says:

In the Eucharist we offer again to God the gifts of bread and wine and remember and make present the sacrifice of the Lord on Calvary. Through the power of the Holy Spirit and the words of Christ, the bread and wine become the body and blood of Christ. The Eucharist is the source and summit of Christian life. When we eat this bread and drink this cup, although we taste the fruits of the earth and our human hands, we experience in faith the body and blood of our Lord and Savior who sacrificed himself on our behalf.

From the earliest time, the Church taught and continues to teach that Christ is really present in the bread and wine, that is, real in the fullest sense a substantial presence by which Christ, both God and human, makes himself wholly and entirely present. A substantial change takes place within the elements of bread and wine. Traditionally, the Church calls this "transubstantiation." This eucharistic presence of Christ continues as long as the eucharistic species (the bread and wine) subsist. We also believe that the real presence of Jesus is experienced wholly and totally in each of the elements, such that, while an individual consumes only the eucharistic bread, both body and blood are received; and if only the eucharistic wine is consumed, both body and blood of Christ are received in connection with the celebration of the Eucharist. The Church also teaches that at Mass Christ is recognized and experienced in the assembly of people who gather, in the person of the presider and in the proclamation of the Word, as well as in the eucharistic species.

For This Week:

I want to remember:

I want to put my faith into action by:

Questions to Explore:

Prayer for the Week:

Jesus, our bread of life and cup of blessing, we long to unite ourselves with you by eating your flesh and blood, blessed, broken, and shared in the sacrament of Eucharist. As we lift our hands to receive you, expand our hearts that we might understand that we are saying "yes" to opening our hearts to receive our brothers and sisters across the globe. Give us the wisdom to understand that our "amen" to your gift of yourself is our assent to join our sufferings with yours and to surrender our lives to your passion and death. Reveal to us the fullness of Eucharist that we might grow and be nourished for the work of carrying your real presence to the world. Amen.

The Birth of John the Baptist

Scripture:

Isaiah 49:1–6
Psalm 139:1–3, 13–14, 14–15
Acts 13:22–26
Luke 1:57–66, 80

Focus:

HUMAN COOPERATION WITH DIVINE GRACE

Questions:

1. *What are some of your feelings about God's action or important stories around the birth of a child in your family?*

2. *What begins to happen in people as a result of Zechariah's being struck mute and then finding his speech at the time of the naming of John?*

3. *What newness is God initiating in you? Be more specific in your example than being part of this process to become Catholic.*

4. *Make a time line of John the Baptist's life and put on it all the things you know about John the Baptist.*

5. *What kinds of words, e.g., strong, fearsome, comforting, usually move you to change?*

6. *Who are messengers you know who remind you that God's kingdom is now?*

Quotable Quotes:

"Among those born of women no one is greater than John;
yet the least in the kingdom of God is greater than he." Luke 7:28

"The LORD called me before I was born,
while I was in my mother's womb he named me." Isaiah 49:1

Did You Know?

The Church's liturgical calendar only celebrates three births: that of Jesus, Mary, and John the Baptist. All other saints' feasts are celebrated on the day of their death, the date of their birth into eternal life. John the Baptist was an important herald and witness to Christ, the true light of the world.

The Church Says:

John the Baptist is an important and pivotal figure in the gospel. He was the last Jewish prophet and made the Savior known when he came. Stories surrounding John's birth, from the announcement by the angel and the striking mute of his father, Zechariah, to his leaping in Elizabeth's womb upon Mary's visitation to Elizabeth, are wonderful and are found in Luke's gospel. The clear and amazing action of God in his coming alerts the community that something new has begun. Some scholars believe John may have lived an ascetic life with the Essene community at Qumran. When he began his public ministry, he wore camel's hair cloth and ate locusts and wild honey. Coming out of the wilderness John preached a strong message of repentance to prepare the way for the Savior's coming. Because he told Herod's brother it was unlawful to have a certain wife, Herod had him imprisoned and eventually had him beheaded to fulfill a request from Herodias's daughter. In his preaching John continually prepared the way for Christ.

For This Week:

I want to remember:

I want to put my faith into action by:

Questions to Explore:

Prayer for the Week:

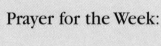

Thank you, God,
for the gift of John the Baptist.
When I hear your message
to repent and change,
may I listen and respond.
Use me as your messenger
to prepare the way for your fuller coming
in our world today.
Make my voice strong.
Guide me in your truth.
I pray through Christ,
the light of the world.
Amen.

Peter and Paul, Apostles

Scripture:

Acts 12:1-11
Psalm 34:2-3, 4-5, 6-7, 8-9
2 Timothy 4:6-8, 17-18
Matthew 16:13-19

Focus:

COLLEGIALITY

Questions:

1. *What do you think it was like for Peter to be called "rock" by Christ, to have the keys entrusted to him, and to live this out in his life?*

2. *What is an image of faith for you?*

3. *Name all the popes you are able to and anything you know about them.*

4. *State anything you know about the Second Vatican Council, e.g., when and where it was held, who attended, and any documents or results of the Council.*

5. *What are you aware of as being the work of the bishops' conference in this country?*

Did You Know?

Paul, who first persecuted the Church, had his name changed by God from Saul at the time of his conversion. He is considered the preeminent missionary of the gospel to the Gentile world.

Rocks have long denoted holy or special places. The various stones in the British Isles, e.g. Stonehenge, circles of stones in Avebury, stones in the form of a large Celtic cross in Callenish, Scotland, and stones at Newgrange in Ireland, mark sacred sites.

According to an ancient custom of the Church, an ordaining bishop who is consecrating a new bishop must, ordinarily, be assisted by two other bishops who co-consecrate. The three of them together signify the whole body of bishops.

An ecumenical council is the most concrete example of collegiality. The whole body of bishops acts in union with the pope in their deliberations and decisions. Another form of leadership within the Church that manifests collegial workings are specific groupings of bishops organized around provinces, patriarchies, regions, or bishops' conferences by countries. In less concrete fashion, collegiality is also manifested by individual bishops throughout the world who show their concern for the universal Church by governing well their own local diocese.

The Church Says:

The faith was spread to both Jews and Gentiles through the activity of Peter and Paul. Jesus handed over to Peter authority for the founding of a church. This is symbolized when Jesus gives to Peter the keys of the kingdom of heaven. Jesus gives the power to bind and to loose, which is viewed as the teaching authority. Jesus calls Peter the "rock," the first leader following Jesus. Peter has come to be called the first pope, and all popes are successors of Peter. The office is sometimes referred to as "the chair of Peter."

The pope is also the bishop of Rome, which is understood as the foundation of unity in the Church. Collegiality is a Catholic teaching that describes an essential element in the ecclesial ministry of the bishop. This element derives from Jesus, who at the start of his own public ministry called the Twelve to follow him. Selected by Christ and formed as a group, the disciples were sent on mission together. Thus, Catholic bishops today, who are the successor apostles, exercise their episcopal ministry from within a similar group created by Christ, that is, the college of bishops. They cannot exercise this ministry, however, without also being in communion with the bishop of Rome, the successor of St. Peter and head of this college of bishops. In our own times, the Second Vatican Council also addressed the reality of how the college of bishops functions. The Council reiterated that the body of bishops is the successor to the college of apostles and affirmed that, "Together, with their head, the pope, and never apart from him, they have supreme and full authority over the universal Church; but this power cannot be exercised without the agreement of the Roman Pontiff" (LG 22).

For This Week:

I want to remember:

I want to put my faith into action by:

Questions to Explore:

Prayer for the Week:

I thank you, God, for Peter and Paul
and their untiring and unwavering faith.
You have built the Church
upon the rock of Peter's faith.
Bless the Church with a solid faith.
May Paul's example inspire me
and the entire Church to proclaim her faith.
May Peter and Paul's untiring witness
and prayers lead me to full life with Christ.
I pray through Christ,
*   who is Lord now and forever.*
Amen.

The Transfiguration of the Lord

Scripture:

Daniel 7:9-10,13-14
Psalm 97:1-2, 5-6, 9
2 Peter 1:16-19
Matthew 17:1-9

Focus:

VISIONS AND PRIVATE REVELATIONS

Reflection:

Meditation: Reflect on the experience of Hildegard of Bingen. She received visions that were interpreted with help from a voice from heaven. Here is a description of one vision: *"It happened that, in the eleven hundred and forty-first year of the Incarnation of the Son of God, Jesus Christ, when I was forty-two years and seven months old, Heaven was opened and a fiery light of exceeding brilliance came and permeated my whole breast, not like a burning but like a warming flame, as the sun warms anything its rays touch. And immediately I knew the meaning of the exposition of the Scriptures . . . I had sensed in myself wonderfully the power and mystery of secret and admirable visions from my childhood—that is, from the age of five—up to that time, as I do now. This, however, I showed to no one except a few religious persons who were living in the same manner as I"* [Hildegard of Bingen, *Scivias*, trsl. by Mother Columba Hart and Jane Bishop (Mahwah, NJ: Paulist Press, 1990), pp. 59-60].

1. *Begin to write your experience and the feelings gleaned through this meditation.*

2. *Describe a time when you have had a similar experience of awe and wonder at God's glorified presence.*

Quotable Quotes:

"   Perhaps St. John of the Cross speaks for all of the mystics down through the ages when he writes, "In giving his son, his only Word (for he possesses no other), he spoke everything to us in this sole Word— and he has no more to say . . . because what he spoke before to the prophets in parts, he has now spoken all at once by giving us the All Who is His Son. Any person questioning God or desiring some vision or revelation would be guilty not only of foolish behavior but also of offending him, by not fixing [their] eyes entirely upon Christ and by living with the desire for some other novelty."
(*The Ascent of Mount Carmel*, 2, 22, 3-5, in *The Collected Works*, trsl. K. Kavanaugh, OCD, and O. Rodriguez, OCD, Institute of Carmelite Studies, Washington, D.C., 1979, pp. 179-80, or LH, Second Week of Advent, Office of Readings)

Did You Know?

St. Bridget of Sweden, born into a noble family, married and had eight children, one of whom was St. Catherine of Sweden. With her husband she made a pilgrimage to St. James at Compostela, Spain, and at his death she entered religious life, eventually establishing a monastery for both nuns and monks. Making further pilgrimages to the Holy Land, she claimed to have visions of the nativity and the passion from the Virgin herself. These visions were recorded and became the basis for paintings, especially of the nativity. Mary is dressed in white, kneeling on the ground, with her cloak and shoes beside her and the naked child Jesus from which a brilliant light shines forth overpowering the candle held by Joseph. Grunewald's Isenheim altarpiece panel of the *Virgin and Child* is also associated with her visions (*Oxford Companion to Christian Art and Architecture*, p. 66).

The Church Says:

In the history of Christian mysticism there are many examples of individual mystics who have claimed a private experience that communicates or reveals the activity of God. This extraordinary phenomenon may be comprised of images, ideas, or words. This communication of God to the mystic may result in physical, psychological, or intellectual manifestations. The Marian apparitions at Lourdes and Fatima fall into this category of private revelation. Approved by the Church as credible, these apparitions are nonetheless not held by the Church to be part of the content of doctrine or teaching. The approval is stated in the negative, that there is nothing there which would harm the faith. As for the recent Marian apparitions at Medjugorje, the Church has not yet concluded its investigation, although many pilgrims have visited this site and found solace and encouragement to their faith.

For This Week:

I want to remember:

I want to put my faith into action by:

Questions to Explore:

Prayer for the Week:

Jesus, you call us to follow you up
*   the high mountain to behold your glory.*
We are dazzled by your transfigured presence
*   shining forth in*
*   the face of a newborn baby,*
*   the magnificence of the sunrise and sunset,*
*   the sheer power of the wind.*
Your revelation of the face of God
*   in all of creation,*
*   in our times of deep prayer,*
*   in the intimacy of friends and lovers,*
Reassures us that you will come again in glory.
You come again, day after day
*   until that time when we will*
*   behold you face-to-face. Amen.*

The Assumption of Mary

Scripture:

Revelation 11:19; 12:1-6, 10
Psalm 45:10-12, 16
1 Corinthians 15:20-26
Luke 1:39-56

Focus:

**MARY'S ASSUMPTION
IS A SIGN OF HOPE**

Reflection:

1. *What does Mary's visit to Elizabeth and the Magnificat say about what kind of woman Mary was?*

2. *Name an image of Mary you want to carry with you.*

3. *What is your understanding of who Mary is for the Church?*

4. *How do you view prayer to Mary?*

5. *How is this feast of Mary's assumption a sign of hope to the church?*

Quotable Quotes:

"A great portent appeared in heaven: a woman clothed with the sun, with the moon under her feet, and on her head a crown of twelve stars." (Revelation 12:1)

"Blessed are you among women, and blessed is the fruit of your womb." (Luke 1:42)

"My soul magnifies the Lord, and my spirit rejoices in God my Savior." (Luke 1:46)

Did You Know?

On November 1, 1950, Pope Pius XII made the Assumption of Mary an official dogma of the Church in *Munificentissimus Deus.*

Mary is thought to have lived her last days with John the disciple in Ephesus.

Mary's death or her dormition, falling asleep, is portrayed on icons.

Zermatt, Switzerland, tucked in the shadow of the Matterhorn, annually holds a gigantic festival parade on the feast of the Assumption.

The Church Says:

Mary, who was always a virgin and the mother of God, was assumed body and soul into heaven at the time of her death. This is an honor God bestowed upon Mary, the mother of Christ. This honor ranks Mary as higher than all the saints. As another human and as given to us as a mother at the foot of the cross, Mary's assumption is a sign of hope for the pilgrim Church on earth. One day the Church living and dead will be united at God's throne in heaven.

For This Week:

I want to remember:

I want to put my faith into action by:

Questions to Explore:

Prayer for the Week:

God of life and death, I praise you.
Everything that has life comes from you.
I praise you for Mary,
who bore Christ in her womb,
and whom you have raised body and soul
to be with him in heaven.
May I follow her example
by responding wholeheartedly to you
in all I say and do,
and join with her someday
in endless life and praise. I
ask this through the Risen Christ. Amen.

The Triumph of the Cross

Scripture:

Numbers 21:4-9
Psalm 78:1-2, 34-35, 36-37, 38
Philippians 2:6-11
John 3:13-17

Focus:

REDEMPTION

Reflection:

1. *How have you been lifted up and found life through the cross?*

2. *Given the context of Jesus being lifted up as the serpent in the desert, what does it mean to believe in Jesus?*

3. *What cross are you embracing now in your life that you believe will lead to fuller life in Christ?*

4. *What are some of the ways Christ is Savior?*

5. *What other titles, besides Savior, does the Church give to Jesus?*

Quotable Quotes:

"He [Jesus] humbled himself and became obedient to the point of death—even death on a cross. Therefore God also highly exalted him and gave him the name that is above every name."
(Philippians 2:8-9)

" . . . the cross, though it has at its heart a collision and contradiction, can extend its four arms forever without altering its shape. Because it has a paradox at its centre it can grow without changing. The circle returns upon itself and is bound. The cross opens its arms to the four winds; it is a signpost for free travelers." (G. K. Chesterton)

Did You Know?

Various forms of the cross are in use in the Church. There is the form we are used to seeing upon which Jesus was hung, St. Brigid's cross with both sections being of equal length, the Tau Franciscan cross shaped like the Greek letter tau, the Celtic cross with a circle that cuts across the four sections of the cross, and the Jerusalem cross, which in addition to the four cross sections has smaller crosses in each of the four quadrants.

Many churches and baptismal fonts are constructed in the shape of a cross.

The expression "tree of life" comes from contrasting the cross to the tree in the Garden of Eden. The tree in Eden, the means of the first human sin through which death came into the world, is the tree of death. The cross is the tree of life.

The Church Says:

The cross has become for Christians a sign of hope and of victory. Through death on the cross, Jesus was raised to new life. The mystery is that through embracing the cross with Christ we are brought to new life. That is at the heart of the Christian faith. Sin and evil symbolized in death do not have ultimate power. God's love is more powerful. God reigns over everything. Christianity involves facing and embracing the cross that presents itself in various forms in life. Through his death on the cross, Jesus atones for our sins, or reconciles all things to himself. Christ is the Savior who saves through liberating, bringing good news, giving sight, freeing the oppressed, forgiving, and healing. Christ lifts us up and is our sign of healing.

For This Week:

I want to remember:

I want to put my faith into action by:

Questions to Explore:

Prayer for the Week:

Loving and gracious God,
through Christ you teach me
that the cross is not only a means of suffering,
but also a cross of triumph.
I place the crosses I bear in your hands.
Through bearing my cross with Christ,
may I one day share
in his glorious resurrection.
I pray through Christ, my Savior.
Amen.

All Saints

Scripture:

Revelation 7:2-4, 9-14
Psalm 24:1-2, 3-4, 5-6
1 John 3:1-3
Matthew 5:1-12

Focus:

THE COMMUNION OF SAINTS

Reflection:

Directions: *Think of people in your life who have had a positive influence on your life. They may be people you have known personally or people who you have never met. In what way(s) have they influenced your life? What quality or qualities of their lives do you admire? Why? Write about these relationships which have influenced you to grow and change in the space below.*

Questions:

1. *Describe how our society measures success.*

2. *Describe how God measures success.*

3. *If you choose to follow in the footsteps of Christ, what will be the criteria by which you will be judged?*

Did You Know?

The remote origins of this feast are found in the honor that early Christians paid to the martyrs, remembering them on the anniversary of their death, very often at the very place of their martyrdom. After the age of persecution had ended, other holy individuals were gradually added to the list of those commemorated annually. In the fourth century, saints were named in the Eucharistic Prayer. By the fifth century, a feast of All Saints was celebrated in certain churches of the Christian East. When Pope Bonfire transformed the Roman pantheon into a Christian church on May 13, 610, he designated that day as a feast of all saints. It was under Gregory IV that the feast was moved to November 1, and thenceforth the observance spread throughout the West.

The Church Says:

All Christians are called to a life of holiness, that is, to conform ourselves to the image of Christ.

Saints (the word is derived from the Latin word for holy) are considered to be intercessors before God. They are not worshiped but venerated for the model of holiness that they offer to those of us still on earth.

The Virgin Mary is venerated, with all the saints, for her witness of holiness and her constant *fiat,* that is, her "yes" to God's will in seemingly impossible circumstances.

The Communion of Saints celebrates the one body of the Church, with Christ as its head. Those who have gone before us, those still on earth, and those yet to come all share in the holiness of Christ as a holy people, sealed in the blood of the Lamb.

For This Week:

I want to remember:

I want to put my faith into action by:

Questions to Explore:

Prayer for the Week:

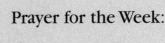

Holy God,
we praise you for setting before us
the witness of so many
who have gone before us in faith.
All the martyrs, virgins, widows,
teachers, holy men and women
known for their actions on behalf of your
kingdom.
We join with them as they cry out,
"Salvation belongs to our God
who is seated on the throne,
and to the Lamb!" (Revelation 7:10)
"Amen! Blessing and glory
and wisdom and thanksgiving and honor
and power and might be to our God
forever and ever! Amen." (Revelation 7:12)

All Souls

Scripture:

Readings for All Souls may be taken from any of the Masses for the Dead See the Lectionary n. 789- 93.

Focus:

PURGATORY

Reflection:

Directions: *In the space below, write your own obituary, as you would like it to read at your death. Use the following as reference questions: When were you born? When did you die? What was the cause of your death? Who survived you? What will you be most remembered for? What was your biggest regret?*

Quotable Quotes:

"Life is not lost by dying;
life is lost minute by minute, day by day,
in all the small uncaring ways."

(Steven Vincent Benet)

Did You Know?

In Dante's *Divine Comedy*, Purgatory is a mountain rising from the ocean and divided into terraces, at the top of which is terrestrial paradise. Thomas Merton used Dante's image of a seven-tiered mountain as the symbol of the modern world in his autobiography, *The Seven Storey Mountain*.

The Church Says:

In our Catholic understanding, purgatory is a state of purification between death and heaven whereby the remaining obstacles to the full enjoyment of one's personal and eternal union with God are removed. The obstacles which are removed are venial sins not repented at the time of death and any remaining effects or consequences to one's person of repented and forgiven mortal or deadly sins committed during one's earthly life. In our Catholic understanding, purgatory is not an opportunity to reverse the course of one's earthly life. Conversion is not possible in purgatory if conversion did not take place in life before death. Since an individual judgment follows immediately upon death, purgatory is that interval after death that erases conditions preventing persons from enjoying full fellowship with God.

It is important to note that while scripture refers to a cleansing fire (1 Corinthians 3:15; 1 Peter 1:7) and burning flames figure in some artistic depictions of purgatory, the operative notion in Catholic doctrine and theology on purgatory is that it is a state of purification, not punishment (CCC 1031). This state may even last only an instant, as we count time. What the doctrine upholds is that purgatory is a transitional state which makes one ready for the experience of seeing God face-to-face in heaven.

It is also important to note that the doctrine of purgatory upholds an unbroken liturgical practice in our Church to making intercessory prayers for the dead. The Second Vatican Council observes, "In full consciousness of this communion of the whole Mystical Body of Jesus Christ, the Church in its pilgrim members, from the very earliest days of the Christian religion, has honored with great respect the memory of the dead; and, 'because it is a holy and a wholesome thought to pray for the dead that they may be loosed from their sins' (2 Mac 12:46) she offers her suffrages for them" (LG 50).

For This Week:

I want to remember:

I want to put my faith into action by:

Questions to Explore:

Prayer for the Week:

Prayer for the Souls in Purgatory:

Eternal rest grant unto them, O Lord,
and may perpetual light shine upon them.
Amen.

The Dedication of St. John Lateran

Scripture:

22 possible texts

<table>
<tr><td>Focus:</td></tr>
<tr><td>THE FOUR MARKS OF THE CHURCH</td></tr>
</table>

Reflection:

Directions: *Reflect on and write your responses to the following questions. How do you feel about becoming a member of a universal Church? What hesitations, concerns, or questions do you have?*

Questions:

1. *What gift does being a part of a universal Church offer to you?*

2. *How are you called as an individual and as a community to work for unity among churches?*

3. *How do you hear yourself being called to holiness?*

Did You Know?

The Lateran basilica is filled with venerable relics. The high altar itself is constructed over a wooden table which, as legend has it, St. Peter celebrated the Eucharist with the ancient Christians of Rome.
(Mary Ellen Hynes, *Companion to the Calendar*, LTP, Archdiocese of Chicago, 1993, p. 166)

The famous Lateran Treaty or "Concordat" agreed upon between the Vatican and Mussolini was finalized and signed at the Lateran Palace. The agreement stipulates that the Lateran grounds are also considered part of Vatican City State.

The Church Says:

The feast we celebrate today observes the anniversary of the dedication of the cathedral church of Rome. When the Emperor Constantine officially recognized Christianity, he made generous gifts to the Church, one of which was a palace and grounds formerly belonging to the Laterani family. In 324 he added a large church on the grounds named the Basilica of the Savior. Legend has it that the basilica was dedicated on November 9 that year. Later a baptistry was added and dedicated to St. John the Baptist. In subsequent years the entire edifice became known as St. John of the Lateran. Because it is the cathedral church of the bishop of Rome, the feast, at first observed only in Rome, was later extended to the whole Church as a sign of devotion to and of unity with the Chair of Peter. Thus, while this feast originates in a particular edifice in a particular place, it truly celebrates the universal Church which is apostolic, catholic, holy, and one.

For This Week:

I want to remember:

I want to put my faith into action by:

Questions to Explore:

Prayer for the Week:

Nicene Creed

We believe in one God,
the Father, the Almighty,
maker of heaven and earth,
of all that is seen and unseen.

We believe in one Lord, Jesus Christ,
the only son of God,
eternally begotten of the Father,
God from God, Light from Light,
true God from true God,
begotten, not made, one in being with the Father.
Through him all things were made.
For us men and for our salvation
he came down from heaven:

by the power of the Holy Spirit
he was born of the Virgin Mary, and became man.

For our sake he was crucified under Pontius Pilate;

he suffered, died, and was buried.
On the third day he rose again
in fulfillment of the scriptures;
he ascended into heaven
and is seated at the right hand of the Father.
He will come again in glory to judge the living and the dead,
and his kingdom will have no end.

We believe in the Holy Spirit, the Lord, the giver of life,
who proceeds from the Father and the Son.
With the Father and the Son he is worshiped and glorified.
He has spoken through the prophets.
We believe in one holy, catholic, and apostolic church.
We acknowledge one baptism for the forgiveness of sins.
We look for the resurrection of the dead,
and the life of the world to come. Amen.

Glossary of Terms

Note: Those terms which display an asterisk* are themselves described elsewhere in the glossary.

Almsgiving

is the religious practice of giving from one's financial resources in order to assist or help those who are poorer and in need. This is commended by Jesus (Luke 18:22). St. Paul exhorts members of the Christian community at Corinth to give alms that they might be enriched by their very generous giving (2 Corinthians 9:11). On Ash Wednesday we Catholics hear from Matthew's gospel—where Jesus teaches us to fast, pray, and give alms (Matthew 6:1-6, 16-18). Almsgiving is considered one of the three central penitential activities of Lent and a work of mercy. (The seven corporal works of mercy are: to feed the hungry, to give drink to the thirsty, to clothe the naked, to visit prisoners, to give shelter to the homeless, to visit the sick, and to bury the dead). The word "alms" derives from the Greek, *eleos*, or "pity."

Anointing

is the coating, covering, or touching of a person or object with oil to convey a religious significance. The Old Testament refers to Moses' action in anointing the meeting tent, the ark of the covenant, and related religious objects with a special mixture of oil indicating the sacred status of these objects. Aaron and his sons were also anointed as priests (Exodus 30:27-30). Prophets and kings of Israel were anointed. The word "Christ" comes from the term "anointed" and is the title bestowed upon Jesus in the New Testament letters of Paul, indicating his role as priestly, prophetic, and kingly Messiah, the Lord's Anointed One who saves us (Isaiah 61:1). In contemporary liturgical usage, the Oil of Catechumens is used to anoint prior to baptism and has its roots in ancient times when athletes were anointed before wrestling competitions. Sacred Chrism, a mixture of oil and perfume consecrated by the bishop, is used to anoint after baptism, at confirmation and at the ordination of priests and bishops. The Oil of the Sick is used to anoint sick persons and is specifically referenced in the New Testament (James 5). Chrism is also used to anoint altars and churches when they are dedicated.

Blessing

is the ritual expression of God's goodness and love. The action has traditionally communicated either the blessings of divine gifts bestowed upon us or our thankfulness for those gifts. Blessings are liturgical signs which call down God's holiness upon people or things. *The Book of Blessings* is a ritual book of the Church which lists several hundred prayer texts that express various types of blessings for individuals, groups, and objects. Types range from blessings of pregnant mothers, to catechists, to stained glass windows. The act of blessing is usually accomplished through certain prayers spoken and raising hands in benediction over the person or object, including making the Sign of the Cross.

Candidate

in the Catechumenate refers to a person who is baptized in another faith and who will be completing Christian initiation by being formally received into the Catholic Church. This term is also used in referring to a baptized Catholic who is seeking to complete Christian initiation through the celebration of confirmation and Eucharist. Anyone seeking a sacrament may be referred to as a candidate.

Canonization

is the process undertaken by the Church which leads to the declaration of sainthood. In the early Church the martyrs (those who died for the faith) were honored on the anniversary of their death and confessors (those who suffered for the faith) were also venerated. Later, exemplary Christians who led heroic lives of holiness were also acclaimed as saints. Beginning in the thirteenth century, the process became more formal. In 1983, Pope John Paul II issued an apostolic constitution, *Divinus Perfectionis Magister* (Divine Teacher and Model of Perfection), which simplified the canonization process. Initially, a local bishop oversees the investigation into the life of the person in question, after which a biography, published writings, and information regarding possible miracles are submitted to the Vatican. The first step on the road to canonization is beatification (honoring the person with the title of "blessed"). If all requirements are met, then the person is canonized (given the title of "saint," which derives from the Latin for "holy") by a declaration of the Pope at a solemn liturgy*.

Catechism

(from Greek, *katechein*, "to echo," or "to resound down"), is a manual of religious instruction usually presented in a simple and clear format. One of the first Catholic manuals was published after the Council of Trent in 1566 and intended to assist the clergy. An early catechism used in the United States was the *Baltimore Catechism*, commissioned by the bishops in 1885. In 1992 the Vatican issued the *Catechism of the Catholic Church*, a compendium of teachings which relies on scripture, tradition, and the teaching office (magisterium) of the Church.

Catechumen

refers to a person who has attained the age of reason who is not baptized and who seeks Christian initiation (baptism, confirmation and Eucharist). One becomes a catechumen when the Church celebrates the Rite of Acceptance into the Order of Catechumens. This rite* is normally celebrated after the completion of a period of Inquiry or Pre-catechumenate, the first stage of the initiation process.

Contemplation

describes a particular prayer form which relies less on thinking and systematic thought processes and more on the direct experience of God's presence. While systematic meditation* may lead to contemplative prayer, this form is generally considered a gift from God and not the result of what one is doing in praying. Contemplation is described by many spiritual writers as the deepest type of prayer that involves the core of a person's being.

Conversion

characterizes the changes that occur in a person who embraces Jesus Christ. Those changes can be simultaneously evidenced in thought, word, and deed. Conversion takes place gradually over a period of time.

Creed

from Latin, *credo*, "I believe," isa pithy, official formulation of the tenets of the faith. The Apostles' Creed and the Nicene Creed are the two best-known examples of Christian creeds (either is mandated for use at Sunday Mass when the Church confesses its faith liturgically). In the course of Christian history, there have come down to us other creeds, such as the Athanasian Creed and the Creed of Hippolytus.

Discernment

describes the attempt to sift through an individual's or a group's experience to determine the call of the divine and where the Holy Spirit may be leading. It has also been called "Christian decision-making." It should be understood that discernment is ongoing in the life of the follower of Jesus and relies on private and liturgical prayer, the use of scripture, and sometimes also the assistance of a Spiritual Director.

Doctrine

from Latin, *doctrina*, or "teaching," is an official statement by the Church of some aspect of teaching. Doctrine taught infallibly is also called a dogma*. In the Roman Catholic Church doctrine is formulated by the bishops acting together in concert with the Pope, such as at a synod or an ecumenical council. Core teachings or doctrines are also contained in scripture and thus the Word of God "measures" all subsequent doctrinal statements.

Dogma

from Greek for "what seems right," this term describes a definitive teaching of the Church given infallibly (without error). The ability to declare a doctrine* infallible rests with the Pope, who does so in two areas: faith and morals.

Elect/Election

is the term applied to those catechumens who have been called by the Church to the celebration of the initiation sacraments (baptism, confirmation and Eucharist) at Easter. The local bishop gives voice to this call at the celebration of the Rite of Election. In this sense, election does not describe the result of a political process or voting, but the action of God through the agency of the Church. In sacred scripture the elect are those freely chosen by God to receive the gift of salvation and to bear witness to God.

Exorcism

is the Church's prayer which seeks to free persons from the power of evil The New Testament reports that Jesus and his disciples engaged in such liberating actions. In the history of the Church two forms of exorcism have evolved. Major (or solemn) exorcisms seek to free a person from a persistent spiritual condition. Today these forms of exorcism are restricted to bishops or those priests whom they specially delegate. The other type of exorcism is found in the process of Christian initiation and consists of prayers and gestures expressing the Church's desire that those to be baptized be delivered from temptation and the power of evil. These "Minor Exorcisms" may be celebrated during the stage of the catechumenate. The "Scrutinies," which contain exorcism prayers, are celebrated on the third, fourth and fifth Sundays of Lent with the elect*. The ritual used for the baptism of infants also contains a prayer of exorcism.

Fasting

is the activity whereby a person restricts the amount of food eaten to only one full meal per day. It can be in the context of a special time in that person's life, perhaps a retreat or an intense period of prayer. The Church requires all adult members in good health to fast on Good Friday as a penitential action and invites this fasting to continue into the day on Holy Saturday as a joyful preparation for the celebration of Easter.

Inquirer

describes a person in the first stage of the process of Christian initiation.

Lectionary

is the ritual book which contains the scripture selections to be read at Mass, both weekday and Sunday celebrations, arranged in accordance with the liturgical seasons*. The Lectionary, as revised by the Second Vatican Council, offers three readings for Sundays along with a psalm text. The first reading is usually from the Old Testament, the second reading is taken from a non-gospel New Testament text, and the third reading is taken from one of the gospel accounts. A three-year cycle apportions out each of the synoptic gospels over the course of the Sundays of that year. John's gospel is read at Easter, on special feasts, and fills in on the year given over to Mark.

Liturgical Season

refers to the various periods of time in the Church calendar which are annually celebrated. There are five such seasons: Advent, Christmas, Lent, Easter, and Ordinary Time. Through the unfolding of this annual cycle of seasons, the Church celebrates the paschal mystery* of Jesus Christ. Thus, the very passage of time itself becomes a holy observance.

Liturgy

from Greek, *leitourgia*, "public works," denotes the communal, public and official worship of the Church contained in texts and rites* celebrated by the people of God when they gather. As the original Greek suggests, this activity is the work of the whole Church and does not lie with any one person or group. The entire household of the faithful does the liturgy and in so doing directs itself to the praise and glory of God.

Meditation

is a particular form of prayer whereby one purposely focuses attention. This focus may be achieved by concentrating on a singular image or object. Suitable objects for Christian meditation include texts of sacred scripture, religious artwork, events in the life of Christ, images of Mary and the saints, and events of everyday life which heighten one's awareness of God.

Monasticism

derives from Greek, *monos*, or "one, alone," describing the institutional pursuit of religious life where individuals take vows of poverty, chastity, and obedience, separating themselves from the world either alone (as hermits) or in community. Monasticism attempts under the guidance of a rule (for example, the Rule of St. Benedict) to establish a life of prayer and work for the glory of God, for the personal holiness of the individual, and for the good of the Church and the world. Different monastic orders sometimes take their name from the founder of their rule, such as the Benedictines (St. Benedict), Franciscans (St. Francis of Assisi), and Dominicans (St. Dominic).

Neophyte

from Greek, *neophutos*, or "new plant, new growth," this term refers to those newly initiated who have celebrated baptism, confirmation and Eucharist. Neophytes, the newly initiated, are grafted onto Christ as vines to the branch and are so designated up until the first anniversary of their initiation.

Paschal Mystery

is the term encompassing Jesus' suffering, death, burial, resurrection, ascension, and sending of the Holy Spirit. It refers to the saving activity of Jesus by which we are redeemed and given new life by the gracious love of God.

Purification and Enlightenment

is the third stage of Christian initiation. It begins on the First Sunday of Lent and concludes on Holy Saturday as the Easter Vigil commences.

Reflection

is similar to meditation but not as intense an activity. In reflection, one concentrates mental activity and takes the time and effort to carefully consider.

Rite

describes ceremonial activity that proceeds from specific liturgical rules or directions. Some examples are the Rite of Infant Baptism, the Rite of Christian Initiation of Adults, and the Rite of Anointing and Pastoral Care of the Sick. Not only these ritual books but all of the rites currently in use by the Church were revised at the direction of the Second Vatican Council.

Rite of Christian Initiation of Adults (RCIA)

is the ritual book in which the Church describes the formation process of Christian initiation. The Second Vatican Council called for the restoration of the ancient process of initiation which included stages of growth and conversion in Christ marked by steps or liturgical celebrations. The four stages in initiation are: Inquiry, Catechumenate, Purification and Enlightenment, and Mystagogy. The Rite of Acceptance into the Order of Catechumens is the step between Inquiry and the Catechumenate. The Rite of Election is the step which celebrates the beginning of Purification and Enlightenment. And celebrating initiation (baptism, confirmation and Eucharist) signals the step into Mystagogy.

Sacrament

from Latin, *sacramentum*, or "oath, pledge," which originally meant the oath taken by soldiers and office holders of the Roman Empire, but became the term used by the Church to indicate its seven foremost ritual celebrations. The seven sacraments are: Baptism, Confirmation, Eucharist, Marriage, Holy Orders, Reconciliation, and Anointing of the Sick. In these seven sacraments, God's love is expressed and grace is communicated. The saving life, death, and resurrection of Jesus (paschal mystery*) is the foundation and basis for the seven sacraments celebrated by the Church.

Sacramentals

are sacred signs instituted by the Church which, while they do not bear the same impact as the seven sacraments, nonetheless dispose people to holiness and an openness to God's grace imparted and experienced in the seven sacraments. Examples of sacramentals include blessings, exorcisms, and the use of holy water, rosaries, and sacred images in prayer.

Scrutiny

is the name given to the ritual celebrations occurring on the third, fourth, and fifth Sundays of Lent during the stage of initiation known as Purification and Enlightenment*. Within the Scrutiny celebrations, a laying on of hands and an exorcism* prayer expresses the Church's concern for the elect*, as the community of the faithful prays that not only the elect but all of God's children be delivered from the power of evil.

Sponsor

describes the ministry of spiritual companion to a catechumen as he or she moves through the various stages of the initiation process up to the celebration of the Rite of Election when the person is then accompanied by a "Godparent." A baptized candidate* is accompanied by a sponsor throughout the whole initiation process.

Tradition

describes the living reality by which all of the Church's beliefs expressed doctrinally, its sacred writings expressed in scripture, and its prayer expressed in rituals are handed down and transmitted from one generation to the next under the guidance of the Holy Spirit. The Second Vatican Council articulated an understanding of tradition as the whole life and activity of the Church which helps men and women to be holy in this world. It is the totality of God's revelation preserved and cherished by the household of the faithful.

Notes

Notes

Notes

Notes